i0

The
Entrepreneur's
Book of Checklists

ʃ11

4

The Entrepreneur's Book of Checklists

1000 tips to help you start and
grow your business

Robert Ashton

PEARSON
Prentice Hall
BUSINESS

London • New York • Toronto • Sydney • Tokyo • Singapore
Hong Kong • Cape Town • Madrid • Paris • Amsterdam • Munich • Milan

PEARSON EDUCATION LIMITED

Edinburgh Gate
Harlow CM20 2JE
Tel: +44 (0)1279 623623
Fax: +44 (0)1279 431059
Website: www.pearsoned.co.uk

First published in Great Britain in 2004

© Pearson Education Limited 2004

ISBN-10: 0 273 69439 1
ISBN-13: 978 0 273 69439 7

British Library Cataloguing in Publication Data
A CIP catalogue record for this book can be obtained from the British Library.

Library of Congress Cataloging-in-Publication Data
A catalog record for this book is available from the Library of Congress

10 9 8 7 6 5 4
08 07 06

Cartoon illustrations by Andrzej Krauze
Typeset in 11pt/13¼pt Berkley by 70
Printed and bound in Great Britain by Bell & Bain Ltd, Glasgow

The Publishers' policy is to use paper manufactured from sustainable forests.

This book is dedicated to both your partner and mine. I know that without my Belinda's love and support, I would not achieve all that I do. Remember to look after your partner for without him or her, being an entrepreneur will be even tougher!

Contents

Introduction

This book provides practical tips and advice for anybody who wants to grow a business. Here are ten good reasons for reading further.

1. **Ideas** – sometimes the desire to start or grow a business is there but the killer idea is not. This book shows you how to generate and test great business ideas.

2. **Wealth** – your own business may sound appealing but should you give up the security of employment? Read how to check if your job is worth sticking with, or if you could do better on your own.

3. **Goals** – what do you really want from your business? See how setting lifestyle goals will focus your business vision.

4. **Capital** – finding the money is never simple, but this book lists places to look you've probably never thought of.

5. **More customers** – if your business is not growing, it's probably shrinking! Business growth comes in spurts. Find out how to boost your sales and your profits.

6. **Visibility** – the easier your product or service is to find, the more people will contact you rather than wait. Discover how marketing needn't cost much money at all.

7. **Time** – you're running so fast you can't stop. Learn how to manage your time, recruit people and manage them effectively.

8. **Payment** – do people keep you waiting? Does it create cash flow havoc? This book gives you new ways to overcome this perennial problem.

9. **New people** – are you simply not getting the best from the ones you have? There are checklists that reveal many great ways to deal with people.

10. **To sell** – if you're ready to move on or retire, see how you can add value and find a buyer, all without letting everyone else know!

This volume is not a textbook. Instead it is a practical guide to the many challenges people often face when they start, grow and sell a business. Each checklist gives you a number of points to consider or tips to try. Some will seem obvious and others obscure. As an entrepreneur, you will already have encountered some of the issues described here. However, it is unlikely you will have met them all!

This book is written for busy people who want a shortcut to inspiration and ideas. It is perfect for you if you are:

- **Employed** and wanting to start your own business.
- **Unemployed** and keen to work for yourself.
- **An entrepreneur** wanting lots of new ideas.
- **An adviser** wanting to introduce your clients to a good business book.
- **In a hurry** and simply want the facts, without the waffle.
- **Partner** to someone who's talked about starting a business but has yet to pluck up courage.
- **Living** with someone who seems to work all the time and is unable to find time for you.
- **Fascinated** by the way small businesses seem to get by with very little cash and want to find out how they do it.
- **Selling** to small businesses and want to understand how they think.
- **Smart** and only buy books that deliver value for money straight away!

Throughout the book you will find that the checklists are illustrated with case studies. These are not lengthy explorations of someone's business – more snapshots of an issue they faced and how they dealt with it. All are based on real people, although some have asked to have their names changed to preserve anonymity.

The National Federation of Enterprise Agencies

national federation of
enterprise agencies

BACK in the 1970s the only business advice available to emerging entrepreneurs was provided for a fee, by banks, accountants and solicitors. Their advice was specific and usually sought only when the need arose. They in turn, referred you on to other professionals, perhaps Patent agents if you were being innovative or Insolvency Practitioners if you were going bust!

Then recession rocked the boat and by the mid 1980s, high unemployment and industrial re-structuring showed the need for a more proactive, positive policy towards building a healthy small business sector. Many Local Authorities set-up a local business support service and the Local Enterprise Agency (LEA) movement was born. The National Federation of Enterprise Agencies (NFEA) was established in 1993, giving not-for-profit LEA's support at a national level.

Today, there are 121 Enterprise Agencies; there will be one close to where you live and work. Each is deeply rooted its local community, with the expertise to tailor their business support services to meet your individual needs. Studies by Barclays show that small business start-ups are 20% more likely to succeed if they seek help from an Enterprise Agency. Not surprisingly (for most of what they provide is free) Enterprise Agencies helped 45,000 businesses and 20,000 known start-ups last year.

The NFEA plays an active role in the development of 'joined up' approaches to business support, linking Government agencies and focusing them on the needs of people like you, eager to start or grow a business.

If you want to give your enterprise the best possible chance of success, visit one of the websites below and make contact with your local enterprise agency. Be sure to mention this book. They are expecting your call.

www.nfea.com   www.smallbusinessadvice.org.uk   www.nesprogramme.org

1 Inspiration

generating your winning idea

10 ways to stop and think

So how do you actually stop the merry-go-round of life to consider your break for freedom? Here are ten ways to stop and think about your career, where it's heading and why you might do better on your own.

1. **Daydream** – something somewhere is urging you to consider setting up on your own. Stop reading right now, sit back, close your eyes and flirt with the thought of working for yourself. Does it feel good?

2. **Ask your family** – parents have a knack of knowing us better than we think. What's more, if your parents have or have had their own business, statistically, your own venture is more likely to succeed.

3. **Check your diary** – in the early days you won't have time for golf or nights in the pub. Cut back on your social life to plan your business. If it's too difficult, you might need to think again.

4. **Break a leg** – OK, this is a bit drastic. Often though, it does take an enforced spell at home to really think things through.

5. **Lose the phone** – try travelling with your mobile switched off and use the freedom from distraction to write down your ideas.

6. **Indulge your partner** – book that dream activity holiday and then while you sit in the bar reflecting, planning and thinking, your partner can be skiing, diving or climbing and warming to the idea!

7. **Walk the dog** – those early morning forays will test your fortitude, commitment and willingness to get out of bed on Sunday mornings. Fresh air is good for creative thinking.

8. **Ask the boss** – in today's enlightened workplace leaving to start on your own is not always unpopular. If your boss rates you, your old firm will probably be your first client.

9. **Paint the house** – decorating will give you more time confined to one room, free of cerebral distraction. It might also mark, in a physical way, the start of a new way of life.

10. **Wallow** – instead of the hurried shower, soak in the bath.

By no means all businesses are started by white middle-aged males, far from it. Whatever your age, background, disability, education or sexual orientation, there's a business opportunity somewhere inside your head waiting to escape.

If you're worried about giving up a good job to start a business, here are some useful things to help you decide.

NEIL was a teacher working with special needs kids. He had a winter when he and his partner Will were both off with flu at the same time. As they recovered, they talked and realized that neither was particularly happy at work. Will had worked in the hospitality business at one time and they wondered about running a guest house in Cornwall.

When they felt better, they had their house valued and contacted some estate agents on the Cornish coast. They found they could afford to buy a five-bedroomed B&B and have some cash to spare as working capital. As Neil said, 'If it wasn't for the flu, we might never have found time to talk properly and . . . well, daydream about the business idea that has now become a reality.'

10 strengths that will make you successful

Starting and building a business is not easy. You need to be able to see your new venture through tough times as well as good. Here are ten things to look for in yourself that will help.

1. **Vision** – without a clear picture of what you want your world to look like, it will be difficult to create. Think about the finest details; bring it to life.

2. **Determination** – you want to do this don't you? Deal with your doubts before you start; usually, once committed, it's difficult to turn back.

3. **Fitness** – you cannot afford time off sick when you work for yourself.

4. **Mental health** – although many will say you're mad, you mustn't be! Starting a business is stressful and you need to be resilient.

5. **Love** – you are going to need a shoulder to cry on, even if you're a man. If you've someone to share the thrills and spills, you'll enjoy it more.

6. **Cash** – inevitably your business will take longer than you think to pay you a wage. The bigger your cash reserve, the longer you can wait before drawing income from your new business.

7. **Flexibility** – usually when you start a business it's just you. That means you make the coffee, clean the loo and pick up litter.

8. **Humour** – you're going to make some mistakes; we all do. The ability to laugh it off, learn quickly and move on will help keep you going.

9. **Caution** – sometimes it's easy to see the opportunities and difficult to spot the threats. You need to be cautious, without being risk averse.

10. **Generosity** – when you enjoy success, invest in those who made it possible. Parties, thank-you gifts and treats for you and your family will all make it seem worthwhile.

Many people dream of starting their own business when they've found the time to stop and think. However, most find the reality much harder to face. You need to be a special sort of person to work for yourself, perhaps even to employ others. As well as the strengths listed, you need a passion for the work you plan to do. Some are able to turn a hobby into a business. Others try this but find that full-time hobbies soon lose their appeal. Here are a few pointers that might help you decide if your hobby could become your work too.

Hobby businesses work best when:

- many people share your passion for . . . whatever;
- specialist supplies or equipment are hard to find;
- there are dedicated enthusiast magazines or websites;
- you already have a good profile in the sector;
- interest is growing, not waning.

Good examples of hobby businesses include:

- bead shops that sell all you need to make costume jewellery;
- classical CD stores;
- mail order religious artefacts;
- photographers.

STEVEN had always had a passion for photography and decided that he would like to turn professional. He knew it would be tough establishing himself and making a living in the north-east. Equally, he knew that he had real talent and could produce commercial work people would pay for.

A grant and a loan from the Prince's Trust enabled Steven to rent a small studio in a recently developed 'artists' quarter' beside the river in Durham. This gave him a shop window and passing trade to boost his work and build his reputation. 'I'm young, keen to listen and determined to succeed', he told me, 'but getting help to rent a studio has made it all possible.'

10 steps to generating your big idea

Whether you are simply too busy to think, feel that your brain is stagnating or are somewhere between the two extremes, generating the big idea is a daunting challenge. Here are ten ways to start the creative process.

1. **Buy a notebook** – keep it in your pocket, beside the bed and even take it to the loo. Ideas can strike at any time. Write them down.

2. **Ask a friend** – who knows you well. Ask what they would buy from you, what you are good at and what you should avoid.

3. **Avoid the hobby habit** – many people feel that their hobby holds the key, but are there enough people who share your passion with money to spend?

4. **Watch the weather** – will your idea appeal to your customers all year round? Selling Christmas decorations or hiring bikes might not keep you in groceries for a full year. Consider two businesses.

5. **Read books** – yes, of course you are already doing that, but read others too. See how leading businesses started, often in a small way. Record what impresses you in that notebook.

6. **Open your eyes** – all around you are people running businesses. What do you think you could do better? You may not want to be a newsagent but thinking about how the one you frequent operates will be a useful exercise.

7. **Stroll in the park** – and other places you rarely visit. Watch what people do. What's missing? Your business must appeal to people. Think about how.

8. **Travel** – you don't need to go far. Visit local trade fairs and see what businesses are there. Pose as a buyer and ask questions. Constantly consider why, how, where and when.

9. **Check your CV** – most people actually start a business in an area in which they have worked before. Don't take this for granted, but accept it as a possibility all the same.

10. **Shake the pig** – emptying your money box onto the bed is the ultimate reality check for the budding entrepreneur. If Auntie Violet has just died and left you a million, your choice is wide. For most of us though, cash will constrain our start-up plans.

Now read through your notebook!

Every business you can think of was started as a result of someone's inspiration. The initial idea will have been prompted by many inspirational factors. Unless you have been in business before, each good idea you generate will prompt a doubt. The battle for supremacy between inspiration and doubt creates the tension that urges exploration. Only the foolhardy start a business without considering the downside as well as the opportunity.

> **MARK**
>
> Newly married with a young baby, Mark had recently moved house and been annoyed that some of their treasured wedding presents had been damaged in transit. 'We hired a van and moved ourselves, packing our stuff in boxes we'd saved up from the supermarket. Some stuff got crushed when I had to brake sharply and that really upset my wife.'
>
> The next week, buying shelves for their new home in a DIY store, Mark spotted piles of plastic crates. 'I wish we'd had those when we moved', said his wife. That innocent remark got Mark thinking and resulted in him setting up, with his friend Jonathan, a business that hires out plastic crates to people moving house. Van hire companies and estate agents passed on his leaflets and the new business was born.

Part-time or Full-time?

There are strong arguments for and against starting your business part-time. On the one hand you are reducing your risk by starting in a modest way, and on the other you are limiting your chance of success by spreading yourself too thinly.

Here are some points you might consider:

Full-time	Part-time
More time for work	Less need to earn from the business
Always there for customers	A danger of missing opportunities
Big commitment	Can encourage complacency
Might look foolhardy	Might look risk averse

10 things to check before chucking your job

Before you throw away a promising corporate career to start up on your own, it's good to pause and take an objective look at the job you might be about to leave.

Five things that might make you stay at work

1. **I can buy out when the boss retires** – so will end up with my own business anyway.

2. **I've a life threatening condition and the company will be generous** – although illness can give you a 'happy go lucky' approach, it may be best to seek fulfilment in your home life rather than become an entrepreneur.

3. **I qualify for a bumper pension in two years** – so why not hold fire and try to negotiate an early release? It's easier to start with the pension paying out.

4. **I actually like work, but my partner is pushing me** – is an all too common comment made by reluctant entrepreneurs. Should your partner start the business instead?

5. **They're currently funding my MBA** – which means that a start-up venture has never looked so appealing. Write the plan but wait until you get the piece of paper before resigning. Next month's lectures should not be missed.

Five things that might make you decide to leave

1. **The boss is a control freak who'll never retire** – sometimes you have to accept that the boss is impossible.

2. **I think they're going down the tubes** – ask if it's true. If it is, you might be able to buy the assets from the receiver and get off to a flying start with the business you know.

3. **I have a personal pension scheme** – so however old you are you won't lose out financially when you're old.

4. **Work is depressing me** – make sure it really is work and not something else that is getting you down.

5. **I've no time to think, let alone study or plan** – turn back a few pages and check out how you can free up some thinking time.

It's all too easy to decide the work is the cause of your unhappiness and that all will be well if you start out on your own. As with almost everything in·life though, you can reduce the risk and dip your toe in the water by going part-time at work. This gives you time to try out your business idea, without cutting yourself off completely from the security of regular work.

Going part-time helps you test the water

Full-time	Part-time
Fast	Slow
Needs to make money sooner	You keep a salary as the business builds
More stressful, it feels 'all or nothing'	Also stressful, juggling too many balls
Always able to respond to customers	Have to fit customers around work
People will take you seriously	People may not take you seriously

Of course, management gurus such as Charles Handy have long advocated the 'portfolio career', where you build a collection of earning activities that suit your skills, lifestyle and income aspirations. For some, therefore, starting a new business part-time, while perhaps going part-time at work, is the best way forward.

SIMON

An experienced project manager with 20 years' public sector experience, Simon did an MBA in 2002 and found it a life changing experience. 'It filled in the gaps in my knowledge and I developed a real interest in marketing. I wanted to have a go on my own, but with three kids at school dared not risk giving up my salary at County Hall.'

Networking with fellow MBA graduates introduced him to people in other organizations who needed Simon's expertise. He negotiated a deal that allowed him to work three days a week for the Council and spend time developing his own business. Within two months however, he found he was turning away work and realized that he could not sit on the fence for long. He resigned and is now recruiting associates to work alongside him. 'It was too easy to cling to what I knew,' he said, 'and in reality I was too cautious. Now I'm working full-time in my business, I've never been happier.'

2 Goals

matching the idea to your personal aspiration

10 ways to answer the ultimate question

Only you know what the important things are in your life. Starting a business is a great way to realize ambitions and achieve goals. You need to make sure though, that these are things that you, not those around you, want to do.

1.   **What turns you on** – this business is going to consume your every waking hour. You'd better find it sexy or you will soon be disappointed.

2.   **Think rich** – imagine what it will feel like to be a multimillionaire. Is it comfy, or unsettling? Maybe money is not your true goal?

3.   **Think philanthropy** – if you had to give away your wealth, where would it go? What are the world issues you'd like to change? If you make a mint, maybe you can!

4.   **Ask the family** – your business must fit with their plans. In most cases divorce is more costly than a business failure.

5.   **Watch the kids sleep** – as they lie there, innocent and vulnerable, what do you want for their future? How will your business deliver it?

6.   **'Take a risk' rating** – ask yourself, are you really a risk taker or will borrowing money keep you awake at night? Maybe a slow, steady start is better than a debt laden big bang?

7.   **Go to church** – no, you do not need religion to start a business. However, sitting quietly in a place of worship watching the devotions of the faithful will drive you to consider your own spirituality.

8.   **Watch nature** – take time out to be alone with the elements. It's a great way to put your new venture in perspective.

9.   **Read a biography** – read how one of your business heros got started. Remember, every big successful business was once small and fragile.

10. **Make notes** – you are embarking on an exciting journey which, one day, others will want to learn about. Keep a diary and record your feelings.

Of course, as Douglas Adams said in *The Hitchhiker's Guide to the Galaxy* the answer to the ultimate question is 42. For you and me it is probably a little more complex and you will find that the more you achieve the higher your aspiration will become. This is the phenomenon defined by Maslov as his 'hierarchy of needs':

- physiological – food, water, sleep, sex;
- safety – freedom from physical harm;
- social – friendship, a feeling of belonging;
- ego – respect and status;
- self-actualization – developing talents and realizing potential.

Maslov argued that we can move up and down the list as our fortunes flourish or falter, but our ambition will always be to seek self-actualization.

> Simone was born in Rwanda and had a daughter. Life was tough with civil war, poverty and hunger destroying her country. She wanted her daughter to have an education and a future. They managed to escape to England and applied for asylum. Paula learned to speak English and trained to be a hairdresser, but finding work as a refugee was difficult.
>
> The Prince's Trust gave her a grant and a mentor which enabled her to open her own salon in an upmarket gym. Now she has her own business specializing in African hairstyles. Her daughter attends a local school. Simone's determination to escape and start afresh gave her the courage to start her business.

10 ways to involve your family

Small businesses are more demanding than small children. It makes sense to get the whole family involved in your new venture. If nothing else, it will stop them turning into strangers as you battle away on your own.

1. **Search the net** – let's face it, your kids are probably better at finding stuff online than you are. Why not get them to research your idea?

2. **Mystery shopping** – once you've spotted who your rivals are, get the kids to contact them posing as students doing a business project.

3. **Visit the bank** – if your partner does your banking your 'other half' will see how well your business is doing.

4. **Insource** – when you start, managing costs is almost as important as generating sales. Use family labour to carry out the tasks you will one day outsource; stuffing envelopes, packing consignments, etc.

5. **Carry the phone** – if you're out of the (home) office a lot and your partner is at home with the kids, a mobile phone will be useful for taking messages for you. Make sure the baby doesn't cry!

6. **Paint the walls** – starting a business is fun. Have the whole family help you prepare your office, shop or workshop.

7. **Fill the vase** – if you're a man you'll probably overlook some of the things that a woman would remember. Ask your partner to be responsible for keeping some flowers on your desk; it'll brighten your day.

8. **Change the fuse** – alternatively, if you're a woman, however competent at DIY, your partner will probably welcome being invited to be your maintenance man.

9. **Book a break** – you're busy and working hard but you need to take time out from time to time. Set some dates, discuss a budget and have your partner surprise you and book regular breaks; even an evening out is often enough.

10. **Buy the vision** – everyone close to you needs to appreciate your vision for the enterprise you're establishing. It will make the inevitable sacrifices seem worthwhile.

Many people will tell you that you should never start a business with family or close friends. This is because emotional ties can make it difficult to remain objective and, as many family firms have found, it's difficult to fire someone you live with! However, many of the most successful businesses are run by

husband and wife, brother and sister or long-term friends. You simply have to make sure that you put the business need first, rather than simply create a role for someone you love.

Protect your relationship if you work with family or friend

- Have a written partnership or shareholder agreement that defines the deal.
- Use written job descriptions to mark role boundaries.
- Avoid intimacy in the workplace.
- Don't show favour over other team members.
- Don't discuss work at home – have a life outside!

MALCOLM & MALCOLM

Best friends at college, the two Malcolms decided they'd like to set up a business together when they graduated. Both fascinated by IT, they established a software business and later moved into internet services. Outside work, they have quite different interests and rarely meet socially. 'We knew we could trust each other and shared similar values when it came to the basics of running a business', they told me.

After more than 20 years, they are still working together and still happy. Their roles have evolved over the years as their business has grown. When it comes to making decisions though, they always share responsibility.

10 things you're probably worried about right now

Self doubt is one of the greatest killers of innovation and entrepreneurship. Make no mistake, everyone who starts or grows a small business worries about their ability to see it through. Here are the ten most common self doubts.

1. **I'm not bright enough** – well, sometimes you can be too bright to succeed. Innocence and naivety can actually protect you from fear.

2. **I'm not pushy enough** – do you like doing business with pushy people or do you prefer to deal with nice reasonable people like yourself?

3. **I'm not rich enough** – one of the best ways to watch your costs is to have no money to waste. Many wealthy people start businesses that lose money.

4. **I'm not good at sums** – relax, spreadsheets and accounting software make the numbers easy to work out. Always take time to work it out before jumping into an opportunity.

5. **I can't spell** – literacy is great if you want to write books but less important if your business communicates with customers verbally.

6. **I'll fail** – maybe you will, but equally you won't make your first million if you don't try. Remember too that building a business is great training!

7. **Rivals will eat me alive** – in fact the opposite is usually the case. Young, small businesses can duck and weave beneath the fists of those nasty big competitors.

8. **I'm naturally pessimistic** – so, you won't make false assumptions and step into the dark without a torch will you! A glance at the downside puts the upside in perspective; just be sure to see both.

9. **I don't take risks** – running a business is like crossing the road. You can jaywalk, wear dark clothing and get squashed, or push the button and follow the green man when the traffic stops.

10. **I know my failings** – incredible though it may seem, we all know what we're bad at and we all underestimate the value of our strengths. No one is perfect and nor is any business. That's why there's room for you too.

Self-confidence is built from relevant knowledge and positive experience. Rather like riding a bike, playing a musical instrument or even making love, the more you learn and practice the better you'll get.

The bookshops are packed with self-help books, all full of techniques designed to help you conquer the world. Few can do more for your confidence than you can do for yourself by simply watching those around you. When you stop focusing on yourself and take the trouble to really observe how those you work with behave, you will become aware of their fears and self-doubt too.

ADRIAN

After completing a music degree, in which he developed his passion for piano and classical guitar, Adrian looked for a career. Lacking the confidence to set up as a full-time teacher, he got a job washing dishes in a pizza restaurant. In his spare time he played in local bands. After a while, when the daily grind of washing dishes was beginning to get him down but a better job had still not been found, a friend dared him to go it alone. His local Enterprise Agency provided free business training and also found him a mentor with whom he could share his moments of doubt.

After 15 months Adrian had hung up his apron and rubber gloves and found enough pupils to pay his bills and enable him to devote his whole life to the music he loves. As he will readily admit, 'I was the only person holding me back; once I'd found the confidence to try, it was much easier to set up my business than I thought.'

10 ways to measure your expectations

Not everyone wants to make a million; many simply want to spend time doing what they love. Checking that your business is going to give you the things you find most important is crucial if your expectations are to be met by your venture. Here's a checklist for you.

1. **Rich or poor?** – if your household income doubled, what would you do differently? For some people, sudden wealth erodes personal values and brings misery. How much more would make you happy?

2. **Indoors or outdoors?** – do you like fresh air? If so, pay someone else to do the office work and spend your time out and about.

3. **Home or away?** – travelling to far flung destinations is an enjoyable part of business life for some people. Others prefer to sleep in their own bed every night. Business travel is allowable against your taxes.

4. **Head or hands?** – thinking suits some people, craftsmanship others. You must choose how your time will be spent. As a business grows, its founder often leaves the workshop for the office but this need not be the case.

5. **Night or day?** – are you a lark or an owl? Few newsagents or bakers dislike early mornings and you won't find an early bird running a night club. Match your enterprise to your body's natural rhythms.

6. **Hot or cold?** – if you hate the heat, don't run a chip shop.

7. **Fast or slow?** – some business people thrive on short deadlines, surprise orders and multitasking (for example distribution). Others prefer a more sedate style of work where time to reflect and think is valued (for example, law).

8. **Dirty or clean?** – like little boys and puddles, some entrepreneurs love cleaning blocked drains or rendering abattoir waste. Others prefer to import and distribute scented candles and incense sticks from mystical places.

9. **Healthy or harmful?** – selling cigarettes, guns or booze gives some people a problem. If you're not comfy making money through encouraging people to damage their health, or that of others, leave nasty products to other entrepreneurs.

10. **Fat or thin?** – believe it or not, some businesses strike most of their deals over large lunches and dinners. If you're a closet gourmet you will relish the opportunity to munch on your firm. If you're a weightwatcher this will be less attractive.

One of the major problems encountered by a growing business is that the founder gets to spend less time doing enjoyable things, and more time in the office. This usually kicks in when you need to employ more than five people to handle the workload. The trouble is that it's almost always easier and cheaper to hire someone to do what you used to do than to find someone capable of managing the paperwork. Crossing this barrier is often too great a problem and many owner-managers (often subconsciously) keep their business small enough to enable them to do the things they enjoy. Business advisers sometimes scathingly refer to these as 'lifestyle businesses'. There's nothing wrong with running a lifestyle business – it's your life after all. If, however, you do want to grow there are ways in which you can structure your business so that you do not lose touch with the coalface.

ROB has had a varied and interesting career but a few years ago decided that he gained the most satisfaction from mending roofs. With his children having left home and the mortgage just about paid off, he didn't need a huge income to lead the sort of life he and his wife envisaged. They also wanted to be able to take weeks off at a time to travel and explore all the places they'd read about over the years. To have this degree of freedom, Rob knew that he would need his business to be either very small or large enough to afford a manager who could lead the team when he was away.

The deciding factor was that his children both had good jobs and he didn't feel it essential to build up an inheritance for their old age. Now, with Rick, his young assistant, Rob mends roofs for people living within an easy drive of his home. He constantly turns work away, choosing to do just enough to fund the lifestyle he has chosen to lead. Rob is one of the happiest entrepreneurs you could ever meet.

3 Knowledge

researching your idea/reality checking

10 ways to research on the internet question

There is almost too much information out there to sift through when planning to attack a new market or start a new venture. Your searching needs to be focused and wherever possible, you should avoid the temptation to buy data. Here are ten top tips.

1. **Google** – everyone uses search engines and Google is the most popular. However, try the 'advanced search' facility which enables you to use more search criteria to improve the quality of what comes back.

2. **Check rivals** – look at the sites of those you compete with. Register to receive their regular newsletter – let them tell you what they're up to!

3. **Search people** – searching the net for the people who run rival firms will often reveal details of their involvement in networks and trade bodies.

4. **Read minutes** – most public organizations publish meeting minutes on the web. This tells you who is saying what about the issues that affect you.

5. **Learn techniques** – there are some clever things you can do with '&' and other symbols. Some favourites are listed opposite.

6. **Ask the obvious** – if you want to know what a word means, type into the search engine the phrase 'xxxxx means', and you'll probably get a definition back.

7. **Join a newsgroup** – these are popular at home as well as at work. News and user groups give you access to a community of people most likely to know the answers to your question. Ask people, as well as a search engine.

8. **Numbers count** – many people forget that search engines can search phone numbers. This is another good way of finding out what companies are involved with.

9. **Go to university** – you'll be amazed at how much new knowledge you can harvest from a university's website. Find the homepages of the academics researching your business sector. Most will have hyperlinks to papers they've written. Also visit University library sites, they're full of free information.

10. **Check out books** – the book reviews on sites such as Amazon often contain enough to inform you without the need to buy the book.

Internet search techniques

Now that you've considered what you want to find, you want to get to the right pages quickly without having to scroll through endless near misses. Search engines are, of course, nothing more than computer programs – you need to tell them exactly what you are looking for in a way that their code understands. Here are some techniques gleaned from a variety of sources that you will find useful. Copy this page and keep it by your PC.

- **Use the best word** – avoid common words and use words that closely match what you are seeking. Enclosing words in inverted commas asks the engine to find those words in that order. So '80 gsm copier paper' will find suppliers of copier paper of that weight, whereas searching for 'copier paper' or worse 'paper' will deliver many unwanted results. You also need to try and use the words that the person who built the site might have anticipated would be search words.

- **Boolean logic** – is a techie phrase for something quite simple. It uses the words AND, OR and NOT to filter results and present you with what you want. For example:
  locksmith AND Epping will exclude locksmiths based elsewhere;
  'new cars' AND Epping NOT Ford will exclude Ford dealers but show you the rest;
  'new cars' AND Epping Ford OR Vauxhall will only give you dealers selling Ford or Vauxhall cars.
  You can also use + or & for AND, and – for NOT.

- **Capitals** – search engines are not case sensitive so you do not need to worry about capitals or lower case letters.

- **Parts of words** – some search engines will automatically search for and include variations of the words you search for. An example is 'dietary' which will also return pages showing diet.

10 good questions and where to ask them

All too often, the so-called experts overlook many of the most obvious ways of researching a new market. It doesn't matter if you're planning a new business or looking to enter a new market. Here are ten questions most people overlook.

1. **Would you buy it?** – if you're selling to people like you, ask yourself if you'd pay the price and keep coming back for more. If not, why not?

2. **Would they buy it?** – obvious and simple, but so many try to guess what the customer would say. Ask some and hear it straight from the horse's mouth.

3. **Who already does it?** – check trade and online directories to see who's already offering what you're planning to offer.

4. **Where is it done best?** – take a journey to see the largest, fastest, best players in the sector you're exploring. Few people travel to research their new ideas so what you find works elsewhere, may work for you at home.

5. **Does no competitors mean no market?** – there is very little that's completely new. Usually it's best to let someone else do the pioneering stuff, then you can do it better. Worry if you seem to be the first.

6. **Been mystery shopping?** – there's nothing wrong with popping along to your competitors and testing out their offer. Posing as a customer enables you to find out how well they sell. Mystery shopping is also fun.

7. **Ask a stranger** – you want to know that people show interest in your product or service and have a view about their current suppliers. Stop someone in the street (or maybe at a networking event) and ask where you can find . . .

8. **Be surprised** – if your business is retail and you're perhaps checking out new locations, ask around the other shops that sell to the kind of people you're after. Express surprise that no one is selling the product locally. You'll then hear all about those who tried before and failed.

9. **Ask suppliers** – why has no one in your area distributed their product before? Get their marketing people researching your idea for you.

10. **Check your instinct** – lastly, does it feel right? Make sure you're not simply seeking evidence to support an emotional wish.

Too often, we make the assumption that making business decisions should be difficult. The most successful entrepreneurs, however, rely on instinct and hunch – it feels right, so they do it anyway. Remember that many of today's most widely used products were underestimated by those around at their inception. The computer, the telephone and the motor car were all reckoned to have little long term potential.

As an entrepreneur you have to balance your instinct against what you hear from those around you. The key to success, or even survival, is to manage risk and minimize the impact of failure. If you try different strategies some will fail as surely as others will succeed. Rather like the professional gambler, you need to have your stake money put aside and risk only that in testing your new market.

RUPERT

A successful retailer of pine furniture and accessories with three outlets, Rupert wanted to expand his business. Most pine furniture is sold by large retailers, with smaller market towns often being the best place for independent outlets. He narrowed his choice to three towns:

- Woodbridge – small, coastal, affluent;
- Bury St Edmunds – large, fairly affluent, close to many people;
- Colchester – very large, several retail parks, diverse.

He paid someone to research each town and gathered lots of statistics from retail units, the local authority and list brokers and so could build a profile of the population. He also paid someone to visit each town and talk to retailers.

Which town did he choose? Well actually, he chose to stick with the three outlets he had and encourage people to come to him from further away. He realized that he had a fourth option – to invest the cash in better marketing for his existing outlets. Entrepreneurs often change their minds for all the right reasons.

10 people who might do your research for free!

You can spend too much time researching. Here are ten ways you can get others to willingly, or perhaps even unwittingly, do your research for you.

1. **Advertising rep** – find the journals that reach your market and ask why you should advertise. They will provide you with statistics from their research and may even tell you about your rival's advertising success.

2. **List broker** – you can buy lists of just about every type of person, business or organization. A broker will tell you how many prospects there are. You don't have to buy the list!

3. **Government** – you'd be amazed how much data is posted on the internet by Government departments and agencies. Ring the helpline and sweet talk someone into extracting the data for you.

4. **Students** – college and school staff need business studies projects. If your research involves a lot of legwork, use students' legs to cover the ground.

5. **Trade associations** – you may not have joined the trade body that represents the sector you're exploring, but ring the librarian or information officer and ask why you should join.

6. **Quangos** – most quangos publish weighty documents that show why they are needed and what they seek to do. If a quango exists to support your audience, ask to be sent whatever is available.

7. **Suppliers** – if you are a distributor, potential suppliers will usually be more than happy to let you have market information. Let them fund the research!

8. **Customers** – if the customer wants you to do something new, have them find others who will also buy to make it worth your while.

9. **Undergraduates** – while not completely free, universities have websites where temporary work can be advertised. If your research pays better than serving burgers, you could get your research results on a plate!

10. **Volunteers** – charities use volunteers all the time for fund-raising and much more. Offer a donation in return for some help. Clearly you need to have research work that people can do easily.

Sometimes, the answer is right under your nose and you do not need to look very far at all to find the researcher you need.

> **COLETTE**
>
> Passionate about crafts, Colette wanted to set up an internet business that would make it easier to sell her work, as well as the work of others. Being a wheelchair user, getting out researching her business was not easy. 'Everything takes much longer and I need specialist office equipment so cannot easily work in libraries.'
>
> Fortunately, her son needed to write a business plan as part of his Advanced Business Studies course. Colette suggested her own business idea for this project and so her son did all the research and applied the techniques his course had taught him to prepare a plan that worked for them both. He passed his course and Colette started her business.

Entrepreneurship and disability

It would have been too easy for Colette to give up. Severe arthritis means that she really needs to work from home so that she can work when her condition allows and rest when necessary. She needed specialist seating and office furniture, together with an ergonomic computer keyboard and mouse. As her own employer, she was able to obtain a grant of several thousand pounds from the UK Employment Service to cover the cost of equipment. If you have a physical condition that makes starting or operating your business a real challenge, you may also qualify for help towards the cost of the things you need.

10 steps to convincing yourself it will fly

Before writing your business plan you need to check that you're on the right track. This is the right time to turn back if you have nagging doubts. Here's a final ten step, 'pre flight' checklist.

1. **Will it last?** – a business is like a dog, it will demand your attention several times a day until you sell it or it dies. You cannot get bored.

2. **Will my partner approve?** – a business cannot be cited as the 'other party' in a divorce. Partners can become jealous of your new passion. Make sure yours won't.

3. **Does mum like it?** – if you've still got your parents, you may need their support later so it makes sense to check they're onboard now.

4. **Deep pockets?** – are you going to run out of cash before it gets off the ground? Before you read about business plans, listen to your instinct.

5. **What does bad look like?** – we all have different pain barriers and it's good to imagine what apocalypse looks like to you. Are you hooked on the good things in life or are you prepared to put it all on the line?

6. **Fallback skills?** – don't get too depressed, but if the proverbial hits the fan how would you earn a crust? Everyone has baseline skills (driving, cooking, selling, etc.). Imagine doing it for a living. That is your worse-case scenario.

7. **The car of your dreams?** – OK, so you've cracked it and made a mint. What will you drive? Where will you live? If you're not a materialist, should you be starting a charity instead? Imagine success; feel it.

8. **Are you a self-starter?** – you're going to take some knocks. Have you the resilience to bounce back when someone or something's knocked you for six?

9. **Do you like surprises?** – the entrepreneur who doesn't get surprised lives with their eyes closed. If you want an orderly, predictable life don't start or buy a business.

10. **Read Kipling** – take a moment to look up that famous poem *If*. If you can read the poem and see yourself having the strength to succeed – read on!

Sometimes however, the urge to just 'go for it' is too strong to resist and you'll ignore the so-called warning signs and do it anyway. As long as you have considered the risks and are prepared to give it your all, then embarking on what others might call a 'mission impossible' is OK. Many successful and established products only came about because someone took a risk and it paid off.

BRIAN

An artist himself, Brian wanted to start an art publishing business that would make it easier for artists and buyers to connect. A modest inheritance gave him the capital he needed and he opened a small gallery and framing shop in an affluent town close to the Cotswolds.

One year on, he is running out of cash and the business has not taken off as quickly as he had hoped. He says he has found out a lot about entrepreneurship and, while he has no regrets, wishes he had known at the outset what he knows now. His experience has made him even more determined to succeed and he is working with his local Business Link to focus the business.

He has invested his aunt's legacy in a year of learning that has probably taught him as much (and cost about the same) as a full-time MBA. Now, he is planning to raise the capital to create and market a virtual gallery, which will supplement his actual gallery. Brian considered the risks and decided to do it anyway. Some might call him foolhardy but, informed by his recent experiences, he is now poised to take the corporate art market by storm. Would an MBA have prepared him as well for the successful future he now faces?

4 Business plan

convincing yourself and others

10 things every business plan should contain

Whatever others may say to the contrary, a business plan should never be a work of fiction. At the end of the day, you will only be fooling yourself because lenders, for whom the fiction is usually generated, rarely lose! Here are ten headings you might use when writing or rewriting your business plan.

1. **Vision** – what is it that makes this business exciting and utterly irresistible to customers, suppliers and most importantly, to you?

2. **Background** – what has happened to you and in the world around you to make this venture the right thing for right now?

3. **Goals** – success will look like this: turnover, profit, customer numbers.

4. **People** – who is in your team and how are they perfect for the job?

5. **Products** – what are you going to sell and how will your products or services evolve in response to customer feedback/market change?

6. **Competition** – who's already out there and how will you be different? The differences are crucially important, without knowing them you will not succeed.

7. **Marketing** – how are you going to communicate the benefits you offer to those you seek as customers?

8. **Funding** – how will you pay for it all and what can investors (if any) expect in return?

9. **Measurement** – as well as stoking the boiler and steering the ship, you do need to find time to check that you're on course. How will you measure performance?

10. **Jumping ship** – a business, like anything else, has a natural life span. You need to plan before you start for your exit. Will you sell? Give it to your kids? What?

It is no coincidence that this checklist is one of the shortest in the book. The biggest mistake people make when writing a business plan is to make it too long. Good business plans are:

● concise – to the point and focused;

● emotional – you want to do this like it hurts; tell the reader why;

- logical- it must also give you and any reader confidence;

- factual – demonstrate your understanding of the opportunity;

- realistic – don't commit yourself to too much.

Every agency or bank that works with businesses will tell you that preparing the business plan is the essential first step. However, they will probably also tell you, if you ask them, that most business plans are filed in a drawer and never again looked at by those running the enterprise. The plan you write therefore needs to be so relevant and useful that it becomes part of your business management. Here are a few myths about business plans.

- I know my business and only need a plan to keep the bank happy – sharing a simple, concise business plan with key employees is one of the best ways to keep their efforts aligned with your vision. Business plans are for you, not the bank.

- Banks need lots of detail to show that you've considered all possible eventualities – bank managers are people first and financiers second. The decision to lend will be made intuitively, with the manager's gut feeling for your business backed up by the plan you write. Bank managers see many plans so keep it short.

- I've downloaded a great business link model from the internet – the internet is full of business plan frameworks into which you can drop your business. However, it's often best to copy the headings and write your own plan, using only those headings that are relevant and ignoring those that are not.

- A consultant wrote my plan and the bank lent me £50,000 – sometimes, consultants and accountants are the best people to write your pitch to a funder. However, their starting point should be your business plan. No one else can really get into your mind and put your passion into the plan.

10 things bank managers look for

Like it or not, unless you are already wealthy you will need to borrow money. In fact building a business takes investment; it's not just when you start that you need to seek funds. Later, we cover where to look for funding but convincing a bank manager to support you in some way is almost inevitable. Here are ten words that will impress.

1. **Vision** – yes, you must show that you have a clear vision and know just where you are heading.

2. **Commitment** – however much money you plan to invest yourself, it will be expected that it will really hurt if the business fails and you lose it.

3. **Security** – as if commitment is not enough, banks usually want guarantees. This often means giving them a legal charge over your home.

4. **Cover** – how big is the risk you're taking? If you appear foolhardy, you'll get no support. The more asset wealth behind you, the more popular you'll be.

5. **Market** – it helps if your banker understands your market. In some high-tech or biotech sectors, or in agriculture, it is usually best to seek out specialist bankers familiar with the vagaries of your sector.

6. **Skills** – your CV, and those of your key people must read well. No bank will lend if your motive for starting is that you were sacked for failing in someone else's business.

7. **Health** – you need resilience and stamina. Invest in a medical checkup and add the report to your plan.

8. **Love** – the clever banker visits you at home to assess how committed your family is. Remember, it's often their home you're risking.

9. **Guts** – if you're too soft you won't chase your debts and might fall behind with loan repayments. You need to come over as tough, but not macho!

10. **Persuasiveness** – the ability to sell is the greatest asset in any entrepreneur. Don't appear too glib or too clever. Practice selling on the bank. You don't have to take all thats offered to you!

More stuff about banks

Everybody likes to knock banks. The fact is though that every business needs the services of a bank and, managed correctly, banks are an asset and not a threat to your success. Online banking is usually cheaper and gives the comfort of being able to check that your customers have paid at any time, even three o'clock in the morning.

Banks are, however a supplier to your business like any other and you should never be afraid to consider changing to another. Here's a simple checklist to help decide if your bank is giving you good service.

- Check out alternative banks if:
  - you find it difficult to get on with your bank manager;
  - even if your business becomes a lower risk, the charge over your home won't be relinquished;
  - good quality online banking is not available;
  - every meeting turns into a sales pitch for overpriced insurance products;
  - your bank seems not to understand your industry.

- You can make it easier to deal with your bank if you:
  - avoid meeting in the bank's (usually ghastly) impersonal interview rooms;
  - invite your bank manager to visit your business for a first hand inspection;
  - discuss business over lunch or even in a convenient coffee house;
  - you take a genuine interest in your bank manager as a person;
  - thank the bank for doing well in addition to moaning when it goes wrong.

- Cash transactions – surprisingly, some banks do not like handling large amounts of coinage. Some work through the Post Office network and do not charge to take cash deposits.

- Credit cards – shop around before accepting your usual bank's 'merchant services' offer if you want to take credit cards. This is especially true if you plan to take online payments.

10 figures you need to work out

Finance is a complete mystery for many. Too many people keep working away in their business and never quite work out why the bank balance seems to permanently hover at the overdraft limit. Here are ten finance figures you need to work out for your business.

1. **Overheads** – the fixed costs of operating your business. You are stuck with them even when you sell nothing. Wise people keep fixed costs low.

2. **Variable costs** – are incurred only when you produce something, for example raw materials. These costs are good because they are directly proportional to your sales.

3. **Profit** – as a rule of thumb, profit is the value of your sale, less the associated variable costs, less a proportion of your overhead costs. Many forget to include fixed costs and thus lose money.

4. **Debtor days** – the average length of time customers make you wait for your money. As your business grows, it becomes vital to keep this figure low.

5. **Factoring** – a clever way of getting paid straight away. The factor gives you the cash when you raise an invoice and then collects the debt from your customer. You can sometimes get 80% up front. The bad news is that factors usually expect you to guarantee the debt and they also charge a fee and interest.

6. **Creditor days** – the average length of time you string your suppliers along before paying your bills. Smart operators always pay the most important dependent suppliers first.

7. **Credit rating** – if you habitually pay your bills late and have perhaps had the odd court judgment made against your business, then your credit rating will be poor and people may ask for cash up front. Specialist agencies provide credit rating reports for a fee.

8. **Quick ratio** – is the easiest accounting ratio to watch and also the most important. It is the total of the debt owed you plus the cash in your bank, divided by the amount you owe creditors. So, if your debtors owe you £10,000 and your bank account stands at –£2000, and you owe creditors £4,000, your quick ratio is (£10,000–£2,000)/£4000 = 2. Above 1 and you are solvent, below 1 and you are not!

9. **Cash flow** – use a spreadsheet to calculate why you need your income to be phased to meet your predicted outgoings.

10. **Balance sheet and profit & loss** – these are reports that your accounting software will produce. Always look at the year-to-date figure as well as the last month's performance. You cannot judge success on the strength of one month alone.

Figures people

The good news is that you do not have to do all the work yourself. Accounting software takes much of the hard work out of bookkeeping and there are people who specialize in keeping books for others. Five reasons for using a good bookkeeper are:

- someone else is checking your figures;

- invoicing is not delayed because you are too busy;

- bookkeepers save you time and hassle;

- accountant's bills are lower if a bookkeeper has done the basics;

- you have someone else who can chase overdue payments.

KATHRINE

Planning to start a family, Kathrine wanted a job where she could work at home and fit her hours around the needs of a baby. Networking with local businesses soon led to introductions to people who needed help with their accounts and she was also advised by her local Enterprise Agency. She spent time with each of them, getting to know the business.

Since her son was born, she has been able to charge 30 hours of her time each week to an established portfolio of clients. Clients range from limited companies employing several people to self-employed consultants. She plans her workload around her clients and her family. When her son is older, she will recruit more clients and build a team.

10 things to include in a cash flow forecast

Your business plan will inevitably contain forecasts and predictions. Certainly in the early days, cash flow forecasting is the most important factor as it will chart the journey to your financial goals. Checking your financial progress is vital if you are to stay on track. People often overlook or underestimate these ten aspects of finance:

1. **Cash** – always aim to borrow or invest more than the forecast says you need. This will allow for slippages later.

2. **Sales** – building up sales, be it a new business or a new product, always takes longer than you think. Be modest in the estimate for your early months.

3. **Purchases** – if you are to carry stock or use raw materials, it will take a while to reach to the right usage levels. Allow for overstocking at first.

4. **VAT** – many people forget to add VAT to purchases and sales and to allow for the quarterly tax payment. VAT can both bolster and wreck cash flow!

5. **Employment costs** – as well as adding a percentage for national insurance payments, you need to allow for staff training, temps for sickness cover and any equipment your staff will need.

6. **Paying the tax man** – it is foolhardy to delay transferring the income tax and national insurance payments you deduct from staff pay. The officials may not shout loudly to start with but can turn very nasty very quickly.

7. **Marketing costs** – you will waste much of your marketing budget on experimenting. If sales are slow you may want to spend even more. Build 'more' into the forecast.

8. **Include options** – the above are all largely pessimistic points. Add some lines to your spreadsheet that are more optimistic. You'll be surprised how big a difference even small improvements to performance can deliver.

9. **Loan repayments** – at some point, you'll want your investment back, with interest. If it's the bank's money this will be prescribed. Include repayments in your forecast.

10. **Slippage** – work out what effect late payment by your customers will have on your cash requirement. Frightening isn't it?

Microsoft Excel

Chances are you're pretty good at putting together spreadsheets. Just in case you're not, here are some top tips for MS Excel.

- A useful spreadsheet for calculating loan rates can be found under General Templates > Spreadsheet Solutions > Loan Amortization.

- Use the CTRL and : keys together to enter the current date into a cell.

- Experiment with Tools > Goal Seek, especially with Cash Flow forecasts. This can help in achieving desired profits by changing product/service rates.

- Remember that Excel has built-in database functionality. With long lists of data, try using Data > Filter > AutoFilter to add filtering options.

- Don't forget the Σ icon on the Standard Toolbar. This can be used to sum ranges easily. Also, hidden in the dropdown menu are MIN, MAX and AVERAGE functions.

PAUL

After a career in health service accounting, Paul wanted to focus on both software training and work for himself. He knew, from his experience at work, that he was good at helping people build both confidence and skills with Microsoft products.

He took the plunge, rented a training room and purchased hardware and software. Most comfortable with small groups, he decided to make this a selling point. Business was slow to start with but after a lot of hard work and networking he found his diary starting to fill. Paul provided the Excel tips above.

5 Investment

how to fund start-up and growth

10 people who might invest in your business

It's always good to get a loan offer from your bank, but sometimes you don't have the assets to offer as security. Alternatively, you might simply not want to risk too much, however much you believe in your new venture. Here are ten people you might ask to invest in your business.

1. **Yourself** – remember, the more you can invest yourself the more others will be inclined to put in.

2. **Your mortgage lender** – increasing the mortgage on the family home is the traditional and cheapest way to raise business capital.

3. **Parents** – be honest with them. You are probably a beneficiary of their will so all you are actually asking for is an advance. Check for tax benefits. Do not, however, jeopardize your family relationship.

4. **Siblings** – older brothers and sisters who are successful in their lives might be happy to invest in your success. Unlike parents though, siblings will want a healthy return on their investment.

5. **Your boss** – if you are currently employed, see if you can negotiate a voluntary redundancy package. Alternatively, see if the firm will lend you the money.

6. **Your lover** – does your lover love you enough to lend you the cash? Would his or her family invest in your venture?

7. **Friends** – people who believe in you might well be prepared to invest in your business. Several could club together to help you. They might also accept variable repayments linked to how well you're doing.

8. **A man in the pub** – never underestimate those you know, but know little about. The man you drink with might well be a willing investor.

9. **Suppliers** – people who will benefit from your venture may not put in cash but might well lend you equipment or agree to deferred payment for goods.

10. **Customers** – your early customers may well be happy to invest in the business then take their return as discounted product or service.

Dr Hermann Hauser, founder of Acorn Computers and now a venture capitalist in Cambridge, says that the first port of call for anyone looking for additional funding should be 'family and fools'. What he means is that those who have faith in you will be the most likely to invest. Those with money and little common sense should also not be discounted. It is a matter for you and your conscience how far down the 'fools' route you decide to go.

TONY

A graphic designer, Tony needed to invest £5,000 in computer equipment before going solo. Cautious by nature and reluctant to borrow money, he talked with Mark whose printing company his employer worked with from time to time. After swearing him to secrecy, Tony told Mark of his plan and asked for his advice.

What happened was that Mark agreed to buy Tony the computers he needed. In return, Tony would let Mark print the jobs that Tony designed. They agreed to consider the equipment a 2% commission on print so Tony knew that after introducing £250,000 of print the equipment would be his.

Soon after starting, Tony won a design contract with a large animal charity. Within two years he had fulfilled his obligation and owned his computers. However, he still introduced work to Mark who set aside the 2% commission to fund equipment upgrades for Tony's business.

10 steps to heaven – finding a business angel

Business angels are people who invest in growing enterprises. They usually want to get involved in running the business and as most made their money in business, that's no bad thing. Angels know the ropes, here's a checklist to help you tie one down.

1. **Network** – the best angels are often those you meet by being active in local business networks. Sometimes they will be watching you, and if they see an opportunity might even make the first move.

2. **Surf** – the internet is a good way to find the national and local business angel networks. These broker introductions between entrepreneurs and angels. Most enable you to register your opportunity.

3. **History** – angels like people with track records. Even if you've had the odd disaster or setback, as long as you can demonstrate it was a learning experience, the wisest angels will not be put off.

4. **Plan** – your business plan needs to cover all the angles and explain simply and sensibly what you want to achieve.

5. **Trading** – angels are really most interested in proven businesses that want to grow. Some will invest in the development of new technology, but only if it's their specialist area.

6. **Profit** – no angel is going to throw money into a deep hole. So if you're up against it and have run out of cash it's unlikely an angel will help.

7. **Opportunity** – have a clear idea why you need money and what it will deliver. Growth for growth's sake is not reason enough; be specific.

8. **Shared risk** – say you've thrown everything you have into the venture and simply need a further £30,000 to reach your corporate climax – your angel will be with you all the way!

9. **Compliant** – you need to have all the proper paperwork – copyright and patents, software licences, insurances, etc. Angels do not like surprises.

10. **Passion** – your commitment must be evident and your enthusiasm driven by the opportunity, not the fear of failure.

If you don't have a good network of contacts, you can often find out about local business angels by:

- asking local accountants, who often have one or two investors as clients;
- talking to business support agencies, who have access to angel networks and can help make introductions;
- finding out who has made a lot of money locally and getting to know them;
- asking suppliers and customers – never rule out investment from them;
- reading your local newspapers and county magazines.

ROBERT

Now in his mid 50s, Robert trained as a general manager and successfully led the management buyout of a haulage firm a few years ago. This deal was preceded by a varied and successful career, which has made him comfortably off but not rich.

Robert and his wife enjoy life, meeting people and helping in their community. They have no children. Robert enjoys helping young entrepreneurs grow their businesses. At any one time he has money invested in three or four companies. His financial acumen and strategic business eye make him a valuable asset to those he works with. He is a business angel because, he says, it is his way of helping other people achieve the success and satisfaction he has enjoyed himself, as well as giving back something to others. His style is to be firm and friendly. Robert is a typical business angel.

10 ways to do it anyway – without the investment

We are conditioned by the media and the banks to borrow money to build a business. Sometimes however, by thinking laterally, you can grow a business without additional funding. Here are ten examples.

1. **Factor debt** – factoring, while not good always a good way to dig your way out of a hole, can be a good way of financing sales growth. Put simply, it gets you the cash early enough to fund suppliers and staff.

2. **Take deposits** – many subcontract manufacturing businesses take a 30% deposit before purchasing raw materials. Could you do this too?

3. **Borrow resources** – don't move to bigger premises straight away, simply find someone with unused space and use that to build capacity.

4. **Save other's costs** – sometimes it costs more to mothball plant than it does to operate it. Offer to use and maintain plant for someone no longer needing it.

5. **Buy at auction** – there is always a risk when buying second-hand equipment, but sometimes repossession or bankruptcy sales provide amazing bargains.

6. **Lease** – almost any asset can be leased, which removes the need for upfront investment or bank borrowing.

7. **Sell and lease back** – you can sell and lease back existing assets to free up working capital.

8. **Extra shifts** – more and more people are looking for flexible working hours, and not just on the factory floor. Could you get more out of your business if it operated 24 hours a day?

9. **Credit cards** – not often advisable but it can be done. Sign up to lots of new credit cards offering introductory interest-free periods. Be sure to pay it off in good time though!

10. **Take it slowly** – sometimes it is only your impatience that is driving the pace of growth. Growing slowly may take longer but it costs a lot less.

Managing the rate of growth is rather like flying a plane – climb too quickly and you can stall and plunge unexpectedly to earth – climb too gradually, and you won't clear the trees at the end of the runway. The business equivalent of stalling a plane is called overtrading. Overtrading is where your sales are growing at an unsustainable pace and customers don't pay you quickly enough to fund your rising costs. Overtrading is one of the major causes of business failure.

You can control the rate of growth of your business by:

- increasing prices as demand grows – to increase profit;
- building a forward order book – of customers prepared to confirm their order and wait;
- reducing your advertising spend, focusing on the most lucrative sectors;
- selling peripheral parts of the business – to raise cash to focus on the core activity;
- referring business to other providers in return for a commission.

ROY SUCKLING

A pioneering aviator, Roy started his own airline in 1986 flying one plane between Ipswich and Amsterdam. The business was successful but the jump to a second plane needed massive investment. Roy discovered that plane builders Dornier had an aircraft repossessed from a failed airline. This was costing money to keep in an airworthy condition. He offered to maintain it for Dornier, fly it and buy it when his cash flow allowed.

To his surprise, Dornier accepted his offer and the business never looked back. Now, more than fifteen years later and after additional investment by a private investor, Roy's company, now called Scot Airways, is one of Britain's most successful small airlines (*www.scotairways.co.uk*)

10 things to avoid at all costs

This book is all about growing your successful business. However, it is a fact that many small businesses go bust and you need to be aware of the warning signs. Sometimes, it really is better to throw in the towel and start again.

1. **No cash** – you never seem to have the cash in the bank when you need it, even though you are incredibly busy.

2. **Paying late** – stretching payments to suppliers only gives temporary relief to what is usually an underlying lack of profitability.

3. **Falling sales** – if demand falls find out why quickly and either sell more or cut overhead costs. Delaying cost reduction is usually fatal.

4. **Tail wagging dog** – you have unwittingly become reliant on one or two large customers and they are starting to screw you down too tightly.

5. **Cash deals** – perhaps you're not drawing a salary and the odd cash deal looks tempting. However, a good reputation can soon disappear.

6. **Avoiding the postman** – you'd be surprised how quickly people get used to those nasty letters from angry creditors. Some check the post for cheques and then leave the rest in a pile unopened. Never kid yourself.

7. **Permanent overdraft** – the bank balance, like a cold snap in winter, never rises above zero. Was it always like this?

8. **The cleaner leaves** – keeping the place tidy has become a luxury you feel you can do without. The workplace becomes depressing and oppressive.

9. **Rumours start** – people talk. If you are struggling it will show and no one wants to trade with a failing company. Quash rumours if you can.

10. **The bailiff's calling** – this is the final nail in the coffin lid on your ambition. An aggrieved creditor has the approval of the court to seize your assets. At this point, it's usually game over.

Going bust

OK, so you have a friend whose business is failing (for it cannot happen to you, right?). Here are some pointers that can soften the bump of a business crash.

- **Liability** – if you're a sole trader or partnership, anything you own may be grabbed to settle the business debt. If you're a limited company, only the business assets will go, unless you can be proved to have traded wrongfully.

- **Directors** – even if the company has flagrantly traded while insolvent, only directors can be chased for compensation. Remember that this includes all directors, even non-executives. Remember too, that action against directors needs to be underwritten by the creditors. If you've no money, it's unlikely you'll be pursued.

- **Guarantees** – when the end comes, people often find that they've signed all sorts of guarantees along the way. Bank borrowings, company cars, the photocopier and much more may well have been underwritten by you personally. It's not for nothing that a guarantor has often been described as a 'fool with a pen'.

- **Insolvency practitioners** – are accountants who specialize (and are licensed) to unscramble and wind up failed businesses. Most will offer confidential, initial advice free of charge. They will have ideas you don't, so don't delay consulting with one.

- **Voluntary arrangements** – these are great for sole traders and partnerships. Essentially, it's a deal struck between you and your creditors, usually by an insolvency practitioner. Creditors agree to take a percentage of what is owed to them over a period of time, while you trade on and climb out of the mire. Faced with a potential total loss, most creditors welcome voluntary arrangements. They often remain your suppliers.

These are the only two 'negative' pages in this book. Read them but then focus on the positive aspects of building your business.

6 Branding

choosing business and product names

10 reasons why people will buy from you

People do not buy products and services – they buy what those products and services will do for them. These are called benefits. It is sometimes difficult to focus on benefits, for, as the producer, you focus on your product's features. Here are ten common reasons for buying cited by others.

1. **Meets a need** – the greater the need, the easier the sale. For example, you cannot make omelettes without first buying some eggs.

2. **Highly desirable** – you don't need it all the time, but right now it's really appealing and readily available. This is why ice cream sells well on the beach.

3. **Affordable** – your customer can manage the payments, either in one lump or by instalments.

4. **Safe** – your product is reliable and perhaps reduces risk; insurance for example.

5. **Performance** – it does what it says on the box. Reputation and evidence of the success of others is a good way to communicate good performance.

6. **Appearance** – it looks good. Given the choice, no one would buy an ugly product if one that looked more appealing was available.

7. **Convenience** – it's there, close and handy. Supermarkets and other retailers score simply by being closest to the customer's home.

8. **Economy** – once you've bought it, how cheap will it be to run? Clearly this is true of cars but it's also true for products such as paint, where cheaper paint doesn't cover as large an area as one containing more pigment.

9. **Durability** – the lifespan of a product often dictates its value for money. The cheapest often does not last as long as the most expensive.

10. **Peer pressure** – if everyone else has one, you want one too. This applies to business purchases as well as those by consumers. No one likes to be left behind.

Understanding the difference between features and benefits is a key point. Too many people promote features and forget the benefits. Imagine you are buying a van. Here are some possible features and benefits.

Feature	Benefit
Carries two tonnes	More deliveries possible per day
Diesel engine	Lower fuel costs, more economical
Weighs less than 7.5 tonnes	You don't need a truck driving licence
White paintwork	Easy to fix promotional vinyls

You must always be alive to what your customers are thinking and saying about your product or service. Sometimes, what they say will surprise, or even offend you. However, if your motive for being in business is to make money (and it should be) you need to listen and adapt to meet demand.

WILLIAM WRIGLEY

In the 1880s William Wrigley started a business selling soap. He was very proud of his soap and to encourage people to buy it he gave away free chewing gum with every bar. The trouble was that while people loved the gum, they were not particularly impressed with the soap. William then had three choices.

- improve the soap and stop messing about with promotional gifts;
- ditch the soap and sell chewing gum instead;
- soldier on regardless, for surely others would soon come to value his soap.

Of course, William took the second option and chewing gum can now be found stuck to pavements and bus seats the world over. He changed direction completely and made his fortune. He listened to his customers.

10 steps to choosing a name

It's sometimes easier to choose a name for a baby than a product or service. For one thing there is more choice, for another you want people to be influenced by the name you choose. When considering names, you should consider these ten points.

1. **Being specific** – there really is nothing better than making it obvious what you do. Economy Car Hire, for example, also suggests value for money.

2. **Positive associations** – link the name to something well known in common usage (so not copyright); for example Capability Brown's Garden Store.

3. **Top of the list** – while Aardvark Roofing might get you pole position in the Yellow Pages, it'll be suspiciously obvious that you've done it on purpose. Better to create a happy coincidence, such as Abbey Roofing.

4. **Generics** – you would remember a business called Wellington's Boot Store. Also, if people are searching for you online, generic names help.

5. **Benefits** – clearly, the more your name alludes to a benefit, the easier it will be for people to remember; Sparkling Windows suggests just that.

6. **Homophones** – these are words that sound the same but have different spellings. They stick in the mind; for example The Sauce Source Ltd.

7. **Numbers** – using numbers passes in and out of fashion. Unless there is a good reason (M25 Auto Recovery) numbers are usually best avoided.

8. **Your name(s)** – although Messrs. Marks, Spencer, Ford and Woolworth are amongst the best known exceptions, it usually shows a lack of imagination to simply call your business by your name.

9. **Domain name** – the internet is becoming more important. Check out the available domain names before committing yourself.

10. **Get a second opinion** – hours of hard work will lead you to some stunning ideas for names. But before deciding, ask others for their view.

Of course, it's not always possible to have the name you want and first thought of. This is because you will be unwittingly replaying product and brand messages you have picked up yourself. Most of the big brand names are protected by copyright, as are similar names. To avoid the risk of litigation, it's usually best to steer clear of well known names.

Conversely, you also want to stake a claim to your business or product name because others might try to copy you when you are successful. This whole area is called 'intellectual property' and is a potential legal minefield unless you are guided by an expert. Here are the basics.

- Trade marks™ – anyone can put the ™ symbol next to their product name or logo. All it means is that the owner considers it to be a trade mark and wishes to make people aware of the fact.

- Registered marks ® – trade mark agents can help you register your brand names and logos. You can then sue those who choose to copy you. The ® says this.

- Copyright © – the © mark means that the piece of work thus marked is the property of the author and cannot be reproduced without permission.

- Patent – patent agents can work with you to protect that part of your product or process that is unique and specific to you. The registration process is lengthy and can be expensive. However, if you are developing something new that you want to protect and possibly sell later, you must patent it.

SUPERMACS

In 1978, teacher Pat McDonagh saw an opportunity to create a fast food chain in Ireland. He chose the nickname he was given at school, Supermac – a tribute to Malcolm MacDonald, then a popular footballer with Newcastle United. His first outlet opened in County Galway, offering typically Irish meals to his customers, as well as more international fare.

The business now has more than 50 outlets throughout Ireland with sales exceeding €70m a year. With a population of only 3 million people, you can see that Supermacs has cornered the market. Not surprisingly, Supermacs is a registered trade mark.

10 ways to test a new idea

Too often, in the excitement of the new idea, people pitch headlong into spending serious money before really testing their new concept. Here are ten simple ways to test your new idea before you've spent too much.

1. **Ask a friend** – this is yet another time when the honest view of a trusted friend can save you lots of wasted effort and money.

2. **Ask a customer** – showing potential buyers mock-ups, prototypes, etc is a great way to involve them in your development work. Show them alternatives and have them say why they prefer one over the other.

3. **Advertise** – running an ad to attract enquiries is a great way to see what response you're likely to get.

4. **Seek editorial** – your new idea might be newsworthy. Asking editors of the journals your customers read to profile you and your concept will stimulate comment and perhaps enquiries too. The editor's feedback is what you want!

5. **Ask ad agencies** – advertising agency folk spend their whole lives thinking of ways to market new things. Invite three agencies to pitch for your project. Their questions, comments and ideas will shape your thinking.

6. **Street surveys** – stopping people in the street and soliciting their views is a great way to test a consumer business idea. Seek permission before doing this in a private shopping mall.

7. **Focus groups** – facilitated focus groups can get people thinking about and discussing your idea. The group literally thinks of the answers you want. Some research companies have dedicated rooms where the meeting can be recorded for transcription and later analysis.

8. **Look elsewhere** – there's not much that's new and your idea is probably being exploited elsewhere. Look around and see what you can learn.

9. **Read research** – somewhere, academics will be researching in your business area. Delve into academic internet forums and read what's being said.

10. **Just do it** – sometimes your instinct will be right whatever your market testing tells you. If you decide to 'just do it' make sure you limit your risk.

Large organizations spend large amounts of money researching new ideas and opportunities. Others simply set aside a 'risk budget' and do it anyway – the car market is a good example of this. Quite a few new car models are developed, manufactured and launched only to be cut from the range within a year or two. This is a costly way to develop market share and one the small business can rarely afford to adopt. Here are some questions to ask yourself when developing your new idea.

- How much will it cost to develop?
- How big is the potential market?
- What trends make me think that now is the right time?
- How will I fund it?
- What will it replace?
- How many do I need to make to break even?
- Will people repeat purchase?
- Who might buy this from me when it's established?
- What am I really trying to prove here?
- Could I do it more simply?

BEN

Having worked for two design companies since graduating, Ben found he didn't like the way people in his sector tended to use jargon to confuse the client and inflate the invoice. He recognized that integrity and trust were just as important as creativity in building long-term client relationships.

He decided to start his own agency with graphic designer and good friend Dave. They called their business 'Naked Marketing' because nothing was hidden from the client. Within a year, it was clear that people respected their openness and willingness to tell it like it was. They have many clients in the public and voluntary sectors and face a great future.

Their new idea was simply to communicate in words that non-marketers would understand. It was simple, they tested it with people they knew and then followed their instinct.

10 design tips to bring your idea to life

Many of us think in pictures and everyone is strongly influenced by images. Your business, your product and the benefits you deliver will carry more weight if they are illustrated graphically. Here are ten design tips to help you.

1. **Pictures save words** – people like to see pictures of products, and people like using and enjoying them.

2. **Endorsements add weight** – if you commission photography for your promotional material, why not feature a famous person?

3. **Sense of place** – the setting for photographs is vital. Choose unusual locations that will appeal to your target audience.

4. **Faces and hands** – make images human by showing faces and hands. Use happy people!

5. **Words** – make sure you use a legible typeface and that the print is large enough to see. If selling to older people make it even bigger!

6. **Colour counts** – green suggests environment, red aggression and blue cold; look at ads for organic products, sports cars and refrigeration and you'll see examples. Choose colours that suit your product, not your eyes!

7. **Consistency** – once you've got a logo or style, use it everywhere; letterheads, website, clothing and vehicles.

8. **Serifs** – these are the little tails that appear on characters in some typefaces. The experts say that serifs make text easier to read.

9. **Brevity** – promotional material should contain short passages of text made up of short sentences using simple words.

10. **Explicit** – do not beat about the bush; state the benefit argument clearly and simply.

The design brief

When seeking the help of a graphic designer, it helps to have a really clear idea of what you want done. Here are some questions you might be asked.

- What is the product or service?
- How is it different from its competitors?

- Who buys it now?

- Who do you want to reach?

- What do you want your potential customers to KNOW?:
  - about the business?
  - about the product?
  - about the offer?

- What do you want your potential customers to THINK about:
  - benefits they'll gain?
  - value for money?
  - urgency – why is it important to act now?

- What do you want your potential customers to DO?:
  - visit a website?
  - give you a ring?
  - visit your outlet?
  - fill in and post a coupon?

- How much do you want to spend?

- What would you consider to be a good response?

You need to be frank and open when briefing design companies. Outline what you feel are your weaknesses as well as your strengths. You also need to decide what mix of advertising, website, brochures and point of sale you need to deliver the result you are seeking.

7 Sales

routes to market, avoiding the blind alleys

10 routes to market

The internet has revolutionized the way we do business, making it much easier for buyers and sellers to connect. However, there are many routes to market – some obvious – some obscure. Here are ten of the best.

1. **Retail** – you sell to the end user yourself. Higher costs, but you get to keep all of the profits. Better still if your customers visit you.

2. **Wholesale** – you supply retailers who in turn sell on. You are largely delegating control of the consumer sale to your customer, but equally you can cover more ground.

3. **Distributors** – these guys stock your product and sell it to their customers. Usually a business-to-business model. Examples are builders' merchants and cash and carry outlets.

4. **Agents** – sell your products alongside those of others. Brilliant for seasonal products and lines where order sizes tend to be small.

5. **Online** – in theory, setting up a trading website enables millions of people to find and then buy from you. Great for software and other downloadable products. The drawback is usually the cost of attracting people to your site.

6. **Intermediaries** – an intermediary is effectively a distributor who does not handle the product. In other words, they introduce you to their customers and you do the selling. Consultancy is often sold this way.

7. **Networking** – some people sell only through networking. They are the life and soul of every party and frequently heavily involved in social, cultural, business and charitable initiatives. People buy because they know them.

8. **Demonstration** – going where people are gathered and exposing them to your product or service is a great way to sell. Someone else has done the hard work of recruiting the customers; for example craft fairs.

9. **Multi-level** – a very successful and often maligned system whereby product consumers are encouraged to become distributors and in turn recruit more distributors. It is tightly regulated and used in telecoms and a range of household product groups.

10. **Piggyback** – your product is sold as part of a package with someone else's. Often, you sell to the other company who gives your product away to make their own goods appear more attractive; for example in-store drinks chiller cabinets.

Choosing which route or routes to market will depend on a combination of a number of factors. For example:

- Selling for yourself is best when:
  - you only need a few orders to meet your target;
  - the product or service is complex or bespoke;
  - you are trading locally;
  - you supply specialist products and services.

- Selling via others is best when:
  - you want to grow your business quickly;
  - established distributor/retail networks already have the customers;
  - you prefer not to recruit a large numbes of salespeople;
  - your product will add value when sold with those of others.

- Selling online is best when:
  - your market is small and widely spread;
  - traditional routes to market will not work;
  - you want to use online networks and communities to raise awareness;
  - your product has a low cost and is easy to deliver.

NICHOLAS

A professional marketer and presenter, Nicholas found that even the largest companies were not making the best use of Microsoft PowerPoint when pitching to new clients. He set up 'm62' in 1997 to provide stunningly effective PowerPoint presentations by matching software skills with sales science.

His service is one that has to be literally seen to be believed – once put in front of a potential buyer, business almost always results. The marketing challenge was to get display material in front of as many potential buyers as possible. Nicholas and his team achieve this by sharing their experience and freely giving tips and hints to marketing managers audiences. Each delegate is given a demo CD and every encouragement to stay in touch. Much of their new business now results from these free seminars.

10 ways that distributors can add value

It is often tempting to try to sell direct and avoid sharing your profits with a distributor. However, unless your business is going to stay small, you will inevitably need to either recruit your own salesforce or use someone else's. Here are ten things that distributors offer.

1. **Customers** – they are already supplying people with the potential to buy your product; otherwise why would they stock it?

2. **Knowledge** – builders, farmers and other merchants stock everyone's products. While unlikely to betray confidences, distributors can give you valuable product and pricing advice because they also sell for rivals.

3. **Shop window** – many distributors are visited by their customers. They can literally provide a shop window to display your products.

4. **Credit control** – by selling to distributors, you reduce your risk of bad debt. The distributor has to collect payment from all their customers.

5. **Stockholding** – many will have warehousing and be prepared to take your product as you make it, reducing your need to store finished goods.

6. **Delivery** – by delivering your products at the same time as they deliver others, transport costs are lower than if you delivered direct yourself.

7. **Language** – if you want to sell overseas, working with a local distributor, who understands the language and business culture, is usually the only way.

8. **Credibility** – if you provide professional services, distributors and intermediaries can win you work by staking their reputation on your ability.

9. **Two bites** – you can have two bites from one market if you sell your distributors an 'own brand' version of your branded product. By offering choice, you sell more.

10. **Feedback** – when testing new ideas, your distributor's sales team can assess the market by simply discussing the idea with their customers.

Distributors, however, are not a panacea for all marketing challenges. In some sectors your distributors will want you to invest significantly in their marketing activity. Alternatively they might only work for you if you can encourage new customers to come to them, which means consumer marketing.

Managing distributors

There is an art to managing distributors effectively. They must be motivated, informed and supported. Equally, they should not become so vital to your existence that they can call the shots. Here are five ingredients from which you and your distributors can create a recipe for success.

- **Agree targets** – the more considered and detailed the targets, the more you will both focus on achieving them. Product mix, pricing, sales per month and level of support can all be targeted.

- **Product knowledge** – people only sell what they feel they understand; provide literature and aids to help them explain the benefits.

- **Incentives** – underpin key targets with incentives. These can be additional margins for the company or target related rewards for their salespeople.

- **Review** – both sides should regularly review progress against the targets and discuss how to make up any shortfalls.

- **Campaigns** – short, sharp campaigns focusing on a single product or opportunity can get you a greater share of the distributor's attention for a short spell.

10 good things about selling direct

Sometimes it makes sense to sell direct to the user of your product or service. Here are ten benefits to selling direct.

1. **Few customers** – if you need only a small number of customers, as is often the case in a business-to-business environment, distributors won't be interested. You will find them best yourself.

2   **Relationships** – some business relationships become very close and, of necessity remain so. This is particularly true for those providing professional services to other professionals. Only you can do this.

3. **Referral generators** – some businesses, for example home improvements, win almost all their new business from people recommended by satisfied customers. Why share the margin?

4. **Instant feedback** – if you or your staff talk to customers, you get to hear pretty quickly if things in your marketplace change.

5. **Control** – if you're someone who feels no one else can do the job as well as you, then selling direct is your opportunity to prove this to yourself. Remember, it's your business and you must be happy with it.

6. **Specialist** – perhaps people will only buy from you because you have expert knowledge. If this is the case, get others to do everything else so you can just talk to customers.

7. **Loyalty** – if you hire and develop your own sales team, they will spend all of their time selling for you. No distributor can give you that level of commitment.

8. **Negotiate down** – you can be more flexible when selling direct. Distributors, quite rightly, need to refer back to you before deviating too far from your agreed trading terms. Sometimes it's right to 'have a deal' and get the order.

9. **Negotiate up** – everyone encounters opportunities to take an order at a higher margin. When your distributor does this he is unlikely to share the extra profit.

10. **Sell extras** – in some markets, once the order has been taken, you can add profitable extras to the deal. Remember, the most important thing about any sale is the profit it generates for your business.

Whether you are selling direct or via distributors, you still need good selling skills. In both situations you need to win commitment. Here are the stages you need to go through to close a sale.

- **Approach** – you need to identify your prospect and make contact. Prospects can be identified by research or by purchasing a list. The approach is the way you get yourself to be the focus of their attention.

- **Rapport** – tuning into the same wavelength is vital. Good salespeople do this through their introduction and through showing an interest in the customer and their needs.

- **Probe** – by asking open questions (those that cannot be answered yes or no) you find out which issues you might be able to solve. By probing, you can identify specific opportunities for your product or service.

- **Proposition** – having established what the need is, you now explain (or better still show) how your solution is the best. Use benefits (what it does) not features (what it is) to paint a positive picture in the mind of your potential customer.

- **Close** – having discussed how your answer is perhaps the right one, you go for commitment; quite simply, you ask for the order. Use closed questions (that can only be answered yes or no) to seek commitment.

- **Follow-up** – once you've got the order, be sure to do what you have promised the customer. Otherwise all the hard work will have been wasted.

The same process is used when phoning to arrange sales appointments. The difference is that you usually do this over the phone, rather than face to face.

Top sales tip

Offering two alternatives makes saying 'no' more difficult – for example 'Would you like us to deliver on Wednesday or Thursday?'

10 ways to sell even more

Selling is not just about technique. There are some additional ways you can improve your sales performance. Here are ten that are often overlooked.

1. **Ask why** – if your prospect turns you down, ask why; you want to know the reason. You will also then have an opportunity to argue your case.

2. **Ask who** – the moment you have the order is the best time to ask for a recommendation or referral. Too many people wait; do it straight away.

3. **Drop cards** – business cards are cheap advertising. Always carry cards and never hold back from presenting one.

4. **Get about** – show an interest in your industry or sector. Attend the events your customers attend. Ask good questions of speakers you hear. Be noticed.

5. **Be memorable** – some of the best business people have a physical 'trade mark'. Branson doesn't wear a tie, others always wear a bow tie. Stand out from the crowd.

6. **Read everything** – once you develop the habit of reading press articles, office noticeboards, even invoices on your customers' desks, you will become more aware of who else you might do business with.

7. **Never stop** – customers have a home life too. When you bump into people you do business with, wherever it is, make a point of speaking to them.

8. **Say your name** – whenever you meet someone say your name as you introduce yourself. People only recommend people whose name they remember.

9. **Signs** – signwritten vans and other 'point of delivery' advertising are good ways of making your presence felt, particularly if you sell to householders making it easy for neighbours to contact you.

10. **Make news** – get to know the journalists who write for your marketplace. Keep them fed with stories about your business. Be innovative and make news.

Networks

Too often, people say they've not got the time to network. In reality, the more you get out and about the more new contacts you will make. Here are some types of network and reasons you might not have considered for joining.

- Chamber of Commerce – membership organizations covering a local area:
  - keep you informed of local issues and opportunities;
  - other members may be potential customers for you;
  - active members are always in the news.

- Breakfast networking clubs – usually meet weekly:
  - follow an established procedure where everyone gets to speak;
  - positively encourage members to provide leads for each other;
  - offer training sessions to build confidence and skill.

- Trade associations – lobby on behalf of and support business sectors:
  - active members hear about new initiatives first;
  - members can build their profile by sponsoring network activities;
  - access to shared data keeps your business on track.

- Professional institutes:
  - active members tend to be the most progressive/ambitious;
  - being a speaker enables you to demonstrate your understanding;
  - networking with competitors enables you both to differentiate.

TOM is an avid networker putting great faith in the random links that can be forged when you meet with people you don't know. A true entrepreneur, his first business succeeded but then failed. He had no intention of giving up and his new business is already off the ground and making money.

One of his greatest successes, he says, started through a chance meeting at a networking event, which two years later resulted in raising £2,000,000. Tom does business with both eyes open and never, never misses an opportunity to talk with someone interesting and new.

8 Profits

estimating and recording costs,
especially time

10 ways to find more time

It's all too easy to fill your diary with things to do, people to meet and deadlines to hit. Here are ten ways to make more of each day.

1. **Make a list** – at the end of each day, list in order of priority things you must do tomorrow. Listing it now gets your morning off to a flying start.

2. **Have treats** – we're all human so working flat out will not produce the best results. Save some things you really enjoy as treats to celebrate finishing the chores.

3. **Check reality** – do not budget to fill every working hour. At least 20% of your time will be spent doing admin, sorting queries and troubleshooting.

4. **Make Friday special** – do not let work spill over into the weekend. Use Friday afternoon to tie up the week's loose ends.

5. **Do what you love** – if you love your work, it will cease to feel like work. If you hate your work then why did you start this business? Sell it!

6. **Time to think** – the old cliché about working in your business rather than on it rings true for most of us. Walk on the beach, sit in the park. Reflect, ponder, consider, think!

7. **Avoid technology abuse** – switch off Outlook put on the answering machine and focus for an hour on one key task. Those interruptions are costing you time; deal with them all together.

8. **Clear the desk** – do not pile up your tasks on the desk or in the workshop. Put things away and only get them out when you are going to work on them.

9. **Buy a stop watch** – time your phone calls. Sure, chatting builds relationships but are you really avoiding some urgent task? Timing your calls will make you aware and better able to choose how long to talk.

10. **Fill the bin** – every business receives tonnes of mail; most of it is junk. Sort it out, keep only what's needed and bin the rest.

Different business sectors present different time management challenges. Often, it is the people you deal with who waste most of your time. Not many time management books focus on this challenge. If you are a retailer, for example, you might be the only person a lonely customer talks to all day – they've all the time in the world. Equally challenging are those we meet from large organizations. They are often preoccupied with office or sector politics

and delight in sharing their theories with you. You need to discourage this, without seeming rude. Here are five ways to get more out of other people in a shorter time.

- **Set an agenda** – if it's an arranged meeting, e-mail over your objectives and any background info first; help the other person prepare.

- **45 minutes** – most business meetings last an hour. The most successful people, however, start their meetings by stating that they have only 45 minutes. Try it; you'll find you all get to the point quicker.

- **Be assertive** – use selling skills to control the conversation and gain commitment at each stage of the meeting. Avoid 'beating around the bush'.

- **Summarize** – frequent summarizing by the meeting leader cuts out excess debate. This works well in large meetings where people keep discussing a point, even though they all agree the way ahead.

- **Steal minutes** – sometimes meetings go really well and you get the business done really quickly. Don't then fill the spare time with needless conversation, say thank you, leave and grab a coffee and a moment to reflect.

10 expensive surprises you face as you grow

When you're growing a business, it's a battle to keep costs under control as your sales grow. The euphoria of success can lull you into a sense of false security making investment seem sensible. Here are ten surprises to avoid:

1. **Over-promising** – we all do it; a customer places a huge order and wants delivery really quickly. To keep the order you agree to the impossible.

2. **Under delivering** – already stretched to bursting point, you cannot possibly make the deadline. The customer becomes unhappy.

3. **Quality creaks** – in the rush to complete the job, you cut a few corners and, surprise surprise, the work is not quite up to scratch.

4. **Slow suppliers** – you pass the challenges along the supply chain and those who've never let you down before, do now.

5. **Late payers** – the customer of your dreams becomes a haunting nightmare. Let down and disappointed, they stall on payment while arguing on quality.

6. **Learning curve** – you hire more staff to meet the demand but they take ages to train and output falls as your existing people help them learn.

7. **Space race** – with all the extra staff, stock and equipment suddenly there's no room. Temperatures rise, loos block and tension mounts.

8. **Systems squeak** – perhaps you've used a manual job card system or rudimentary accounts software. All this extra work means you need to upgrade.

9. **Time travels** – the hands on the clock seem to go round faster and faster and there's never time for anything.

10. **Partner's panic** – all of a sudden, just when everything that can go wrong seems to, you get home and are met with a barrage of anxious questions from the love of your life.

Of course, growing a business is not all bad news. You simply have to be alert to the fact that unless you've been out and invested in people, plant and processes before winning those extra sales, it's going to be tough for a while. Building a business can be rather like playing a computer game. As you complete each stage successfully, the next seems to be that little bit harder and the spooks are all moving that much faster.

Here are some of the positive things you can do to limit the downside of growth.

- **Schedule** – scheduling your work, using specialist software, a spreadsheet or even a calendar on the wall, enables you to allocate time and resources and to plan when things are needed. Tell customers when their job is scheduled so they know when you expect to deliver.

- **Communicate** – think about how leading e-commerce sites like Amazon e-mail to confirm your order and expected delivery, and then again when the order is despatched. If there's a problem you are informed straight away. You cannot be angry because you are kept informed; the firm is honest and realistic. Think how you could communicate more effectively.

- **Evaluate** – take time to look back on each job you do. Did you complete it within the budgeted material cost and time? (Did you measure the time it took?) Only by looking at what has happened can you change what will happen in the future. Create a culture of continuous improvement.

HELEN manages and runs a business concerned with luxury ski chalets in the French Alps. Her customers tend to be successful people and can, she says, be very discerning. Very much a perfectionist, Helen enjoyed predicting and planning for every possible eventuality.

However, this has made it difficult to grow the business as she was always so busy. She made time to network with other business people so that she could understand how they managed to grow their businesses. Helen found that while it was nice to give a Rolls Royce service, most customers were just as happy with less.

By focusing on the aspects of service that her customers value most, she has found time to do more. Helen's business has started to grow.

10 ways to work out your true costs

As businesses grow it's not unusual for the cost structure to change. You also find you need to do things differently, perhaps even outsourcing some operations. This means that your cost base can change. Here are ten ways to make sure you know what your costs really are.

1. **Timesheets** – these are hard to introduce when you've never used them before. However, recording the time spent on each job by each person is the only way to see where the time goes. Keep timesheets from day one?

2. **Budget** – create a detailed budget for your business. Know how much you expect to sell and how much you expect it will cost to deliver.

3. **Overheads** – spread these over the year and build them into your estimates.

4. **Mark-up** – many businesses like to roll all of their costs into a mark-up on their time; car repair workshops are a good example. Check your next bill.

5. **Finance** – it's easy to overlook bank and interest charges, plus loan arrangement fees in your overhead costs. Don't forget them.

6. **Bad debts** – if you suffer from bad debts, build a figure into your pricing so that all customers are covering the occasional non-payer.

7. **Good buying** – make one person responsible for buying. It keeps it simple and stops everyone ordering stuff you can't track.

8. **Purchase orders** – having a piece of paper your bookkeeper can match with a supplier invoice prevents mistakes.

9. **Add what's new** – if you've not looked at your costs lately, particularly your overheads, add in the new costs. Update whenever things change.

10. **Benchmark** – find others in your business sector and share data; find out where their costs are lower. Pick those you don't directly compete with.

As a business grows, it moves from being informal to organized, or at least it should! In the early days, the founder usually keeps everything in their head. As activity grows, this becomes harder and systems are needed. Setting up systems can be quite a headache for it means analysing what has been going on in the business. To start with things change quickly.

For many owner managers the hardest thing is letting go. To trust someone else to make purchasing decisions, estimate jobs and prepare invoices is a big step to take. It is even harder when you realize that it's their job and your house that may be on the line. This is the time when management skills develop rapidly as things suddenly get bigger.

Another common concern is that in the early days, profitability is high for overheads are limited and everyone is directly concerned with making and selling. Systems sap profits and, in almost every case, profit falls as a percentage of sales. Seeing this coming, many entrepreneurs step off the treadmill and stay small. However, entrepreneurship is not just about making profit, it's about building value into a business which you can sell one day. Efficient systems and well managed businesses that no longer depend on their founder are businesses that can be sold.

TERRY & JON

Colleagues in a financial services company, Terry and Jon wanted to start their own business. 'ZoomZoom' was the product of their planning. The company builds websites and provides e-commerce solutions to other small businesses.

In the early years, they just did the work and sent the client an invoice. They made a living but the business never seemed to have the cash it needed for investment in better equipment, new people and marketing.

Then they created themselves an intranet where all costs and time are recorded, job by job. They found that by knowing when a project was going over budget, they could ask the client to pay more. Profitability become the norm rather than the exception and the business is now growing. The system they have developed for themselves has been purchased by others. It has become a product in its own right.

10 extras to put on the bill

With so many of the things we buy it is the extras that make the provider their profit. What's more, it is often the optional extras that differentiate the product in the marketplace. Cars and first class travel are good examples. Here are ten extras almost any business can offer.

1. **Morning delivery** – people will pay extra for quicker delivery. All you do is rearrange your driver's route to go there first.

2. **Changes** – every time a customer has a change of mind, it creates work. Even if it doesn't, make it obvious it's a change and charge for it.

3. **Overtime** – if you have to incur higher labour costs to meet customers' deadlines, should they not pay more?

4. **Assembly** – so many people just do what they always do and forget to look for opportunities. If you make components why not see if you can handle assembly as well.

5. **Disbursements** – solicitors have a wonderful way of recording every phone call and postage stamp; and then calling them disbursements and charging. Do the same.

6. **Packaging** – environmental legislation makes packaging disposal a real headache for many. If you make regular deliveries, collect used packaging and recycle or reuse.

7. **Just ask** – Indian restaurants seem to offer you extras instinctively; poppadoms, pickles, side dishes, more beer. They understand that the more you ask, the more you get.

8. **Assume** – add things to the order and give the customer the chance to opt out; most will buy. A good example is the travel insurance added by online rail ticket sellers.

9. **Time** – time is your biggest cost. If a job is completed in less time than you estimated do not automatically pass the saving on to the customer.

10. **Offer choices** – even if two options cost you the same, you can always ask more for the most popular. Price should be linked to demand, not your costs.

The golden rule when pricing your work is to always base your price on market conditions. Too many people simply tally up their costs and add a margin. You will find that if you set your prices to reflect market conditions, some things you make or sell will earn you more than others. That's fine and, at times, you can use part of this extra margin to encourage people to try new products. This is achieved by offering 'buy one get one free' or similar deals.

You therefore need a range of products or services to be able to give your customers choice. By giving choices, you make it harder for them to say no.

Your product or service ranges should contain:

- a low cost, entry level option – allows new customers a low risk trial;
- a high cost, top flight option – makes everything else look better value;
- a mid-range cost with choice of options – where most of your work is done;
- optional extras – profit laden add-ons.

More examples of adding extras

Product or service	High margin added extra
Bicycle hire	Maps
Pre-mixed concrete	Shuttering
Hotel	Flowers and chocolates in room
Car maintenance	Valeting

Remember that you can always discount extras from time to time to create incentives.

9 Taxes

expecting the often unexpected

10 taxes you need to know about

Nobody likes paying taxes but, unless your business is a failure, taxes will form part of your business life. Taxes also have a habit of changing, so do not act on anything you read on this page. Use these notes as a checklist and seek professional advice. Here are ten basics you may not yet know.

1. **Income tax** – is what you will have paid at some point as an employee. It is deducted from your pay and sent to the Inland Revenue on your behalf. As an employer you do the deducting and sending. It's rarely worth calculating yourself; use a bureau service instead.

2. **Self-assessment** – is what you do as a self-employed person or partner in an unincorporated firm. You then pay your income tax in two lumps, in January and June. Most people pay an accountant to handle this.

3. **National insurance** – this tax affects both employees and employers. Employers pay this to the Inland Revenue. Never be tempted to make them wait for tax payments; tax officials can get very angry very quickly!

4. **VAT** – if your sales exceed a certain threshold, you have to register for and charge VAT. This can be a real problem if you sell to consumers who cannot reclaim the tax as a business might. However, once registered you can reclaim VAT that others charge you.

5. **Business rates** – this tax is charged on business premises and collected by the local authority.

6. **Corporation tax** – limited companies and PLCs pay this. It is levied on profits and can be reduced by investing in equipment that can be depreciated against the tax liability.

7. **Cars and vans** – if you are a director or employee of your business and the business runs your car, you will be taxed on it as a 'benefit in kind'. If you are self-employed, the deal is usually better. If you use your own car in your business, you can pay yourself certain tax free allowances.

8. **Expenses** – while it is quite acceptable to reimburse most legitimate business expenses free of tax, avoid the temptation to cheat. It's not worth the risk.

9. **Overseas** – when you buy or sell outside the UK, particularly outside Europe, you may incur additional tax liabilities. Within Europe it's usually like the UK.

10. **Cash** – some sectors of the economy seem to delight in trading in cash and not declaring all their income to the taxman. Before you get tempted, check out the penalties and see if you really want to take the risk.

Accountants

The cost of a good accountant is almost always recouped by the amount of tax saved. Trouble is, you get to see the bill so sometimes it hurts. Choosing the right accountant for you and your business is really important. Here are some pointers to help you find the best for you.

- Recommendation – ask people you like and respect who they use and why.

- Local – it's usually best to choose someone nearby; it's easier to visit.

- Appropriate – choose an accountant who works with businesses of the size you plan to be. This makes it less likely you'll outgrow your accountant.

- Values – we all have different values, attitudes and opinions. Choosing one that thinks the way you do will help you both get on.

- Price – don't buy on price; cheapest isn't always best.

10 pertinent points about business structure

You should not structure your business solely to reduce tax. There are other equally important things to take into account.

1. **Risk** – if your business operates in fields where financial risks are high, it will be better to protect yourself by setting up a 'limited liability' company. This literally limits your personal liability, unless you have acted wrongfully.

2. **Reward** – how much money do you expect, or want, to make? The size of your ambition will influence the way your business is structured.

3. **People** – if there are several of you, setting up a limited company allows you to apportion shares in line with investment or ownership. What's more, dividends (profits distributed to shareholders) can be a fair way to reward yourselves.

4. **For sale?** – limited companies, because their accounting is reported to Companies House, are easier to sell because trading is more transparent.

5. **Want simple?** – being self-employed (a sole trader) is the simplest business structure; it's just you and an annual tax return to complete.

6. **Don't divorce** – not a pleasant thought, but if you put half of your business in your partner's name to save tax you'll have a problem if you separate.

7. **Later on** – the tax treatment of the proceeds from the sale of business shares and assets often makes creating a company a good move. Take advice.

8. **Customer perception** – in some marketplaces, you are not taken seriously unless you have a limited company. This is perhaps rather silly but true all the same. You must decide if you are going to make a stand or follow the herd.

9. **Trading name** – even if you decide to set up a limited company, you can still use a memorable trading name. If the name you want is not registrable, you may still be able to be ABC Ltd., trading as Alphabets.

10. **Reputation** – just to remind you that what you do, and how others see your business, is actually more important than how you set the business up!

Some people go to extraordinary lengths to make their business appear to be something it isn't. This often has as much to do with their feelings of insecurity as any practical need. Here are some dos and don'ts about making your business look real.

- **You** – in most small businesses, like it or not, you are the business. How you behave and indeed your level of confidence, will say most about the firm.

- **Phone** – answering the phone professionally, without background noises from children, the TV or your pet parrot, suggests you are on the ball.

- **Phone 2** – if you work from home, invest in a separate business line and either buy an answering machine or get calls forwarded when you're out.

- **e-mail** – domain names are so cheap now that there really is no excuse for being yourco@hotmail.com.

- **Address** – as long as you make sure you use your postcode and talk nicely to your postman, you can drop '147 Station Road', and replace it with YourCo, Station Road.

RICHARD

A talented graphic designer and photographer, Richard couldn't afford to rent a studio when he started his business, preferring instead to invest in a top of the range Apple Mac computer. He lived in a flat in a nice part of the city and decided to change his address to 'Studio 5, 123 The Street.' By calling his flat a studio and meeting his clients at their office, he saved money he would have spent in rent. He was also able to work when it suited him without having to leave home.

When his business had grown enough to employ an assistant, he did a deal with a client moving into an empty office at their place and offsetting their work against the rent. This way, he also secured the long-term support of a key client.

10 ways to save your customers money and make more yourself

Your goal as an entrepreneur is to generate profits and build value into your business. You do not need to chase turnover for the sake of it. Remember the old adage 'turnover is vanity, profit is sanity'. Here then, are ten ways you can work smarter, not harder.

1. **Earn commission** – faced with a bigger deal than you can comfortably manage? Save yourself the worry; let your supplier deal direct and then charge commission on the deal.

2. **Labour only** – many small builders ask their customer to visit the builders' merchant and they simply supply labour. Because they stay below the VAT registration threshold, they can charge more for their time and be cheaper.

3. **Project manage** – if you're really busy then, rather than growing the business, focus on selling your expertise and subcontract what you used to do.

4. **Work from home** – offices may make you feel more businesslike, but are you there enough to make the investment worthwhile? Save the expense; charge a little less and make a little more.

5. **Virtual PA** – telecoms technology means your phone can be answered, messages taken and admin work done by people who themselves work from home and are there when you need them. Delay hiring staff until it's vital.

6. **Simplify** – people often want the solution they've seen on TV or read of in the press. By showing customers a simpler solution, you can save them money and not be under price pressure yourself.

7. **Teach, don't do** – charging your clients to do a task themselves will make you more money in the long run. You have more time for more customers.

8. **Maintenance agreements** – are not just for IT companies. Who would pay you a monthly fee and call you when they need you?

9. **Two birds/one stone** – encouraging people to share you will, through economies of scale, save money. That saving can be shared with you.

10. **Recycle** – avoid reinventing the wheel. Sell identical things to similar people and reduce your costly learning curve.

Businesses grow by doing bigger jobs and by doing more jobs of the same size. Both routes have merit, but sometimes your sense of loyalty to your earliest clients makes it hard to leave them when bigger and better work is on offer elsewhere. Often, especially with customers who remember growing their own business, simply sharing the challenge will enable you to move on. Sometimes, when they realize they are holding you back, your oldest customers will find really creative ways of remaining your most profitable account.

80:20 rule

Every business textbook talks about the 80:20 rule. The phrase was coined by Pareto and suggests that 80% of the profit came from 20% of the customers. Your challenge is to recognize who's making you the money, find more customers like them and discourage those who give you lots of heartache and little return.

DAVE

A graphic designer, Dave started a business with his friend Ben. They handled the advertising for a local coach company, placing ads and taking a 10% commission from the publications. With many excursions, holidays and small local publications, they soon found they were doing lots of work for little return. Worse still was that much of the advertising did not require them to design new artwork – so no profit there.

They worked out that all they needed to do was design one brochure containing 9 hours of design work to equal the margin that almost 30 hours of disruptive, urgent advert placement was earning. They politely shared this with the client who now handles the advertising alone.

10 risks you can cover with insurance

Entrepreneurship is about risk. But some risks can be reduced, or at least minimized through insurance and other financial techniques. Here are ten things you should consider.

1. **Car** – if you own a car and use it for your business, well done; this is usually the most tax efficient way to travel. However, make sure your insurance covers business journeys as well as the usual 'social, domestic and pleasure'.

2. **Office** – if you work from home, there are some super SoHo (small office, home office) products that bundle together all you need. Make sure you insure essential equipment.

3. **Premises** – if you operate from a business address, make sure it's insured. Check with your landlord to see what he covers. Plug the gaps.

4. **People** – every business needs public liability cover. If you employ people, even if only a part-time cleaner, you need employer's liability cover.

5. **Your advice** – professional indemnity insurance is something you may never need but should have anyway. Professional bodies often provide this cheaply to their members. In the public sector cover is often a condition of contract.

6. **Your health** – however much you admire public health services, you need to get fixed quick if you're ill; private medical cover usually makes sense.

7. **Your income** – calculate your minimum survival budget and buy insurance to provide that should you become long-term sick.

8. **Your life** – cover the business debts with term life assurance. That way, if you die, your successors start with a clean slate.

9. **Partners** – if you have partners or fellow directors, make sure that everyone is insured for all of the above. It avoids difficult decisions when one of you is ill.

10. **Your future** – make sure you enjoy life to the full but be kind to yourself; eat well, keep fit and avoid stress. Well-being cannot be covered by insurance but is important all the same!

BUYING INSURANCE

There is an old saying that 'no one has endurance like a man who sells insurance'. The persistent nature of insurance salespeople, the determination of banks to sell you cover, together with the almost daily direct mail assaults we all receive from insurers, immunizes us from the desire to sort it out. The insurance industry tries too hard and this puts us all off.

However, when buying insurance there are some short cuts to finding the right people. Good places to look are:

- Membership organizations – these often have special deals struck with insurers on behalf of their members. Check them out.

- On-line – some online communities that cater for people like you will also have access to competitive deals. These often have special deals struck with insurers and pass savings on to their membership.

- www – an internet search will find good insurers; some sectors, such as motor, do much of their business over the internet.

- Broker – for simplicity, putting your business with one broker means that you don't have to spend time chasing quotes and comparing deals. Brokers also make claims easier to manage.

- The doormat – yes, sometimes those offers that drop through the letterbox are worth taking up.

SIMON

It should never be forgotten that insurance businesses can be entrepreneurial too. After a corporate sales career, Simon set up 'Trade Credit Solutions' to help other business people reduce the danger of financial catastrophe. Simon sells insurance cover that protects companies from bad debt, currency fluctuations and some of the political uncertainties that can jeopardize export trade.

As Simon says, 'almost any business risk can be insured. It's simply a matter of finding someone to take that risk for an acceptable premium.'

10 Cash flow

keeping the ship afloat

10 things bank managers like to hear

Bank managers are not entrepreneurs. You have to overcome the natural cultural boundary between their nice safe corporate world and your more exciting, volatile one. Here are ten words you can use to reassure them.

1. **Sacrifice** – give up an expensive, health endangering pastime and promise to spend the time on your cash flow forecast instead.

2. **Sell me more** – bank managers have sales targets; let yours sell you something that's not too expensive and that might be useful. Use it as a lever to reduce bank charges.

3. **Lunch?** – treat your bank manager to regular, modest lunches. Encourage open, frank and personal conversation; become a friend.

4. **Caution** – better to be seen to be cautious than rash.

5. **Good news** – always share good news. It gets filed and remembered when problems occur; you need all the positives you can get then!

6. **We had a problem** – sort problems and then mention in passing how you managed it; and point out that the thing your bank worries about didn't actually happen.

7. **Meet my friend** – like anyone in business, banks welcome referrals. Sometimes they refer customers to each other as well.

8. **We've won** – let's face it, life in a bank can be pretty routine. Enter and win a promotion for a business award and invite your bank manager to the party.

9. **Here are the figures** – in case you've not realized it, bank software calculates all sorts of statistics from the activity on your account. Send monthly management accounts to show that you know as much as they do.

10. **I want to expand** – you're doing well and everything's hunky-dory. Your bank manager would love to lend you some more money. Remember, bank managers have targets too!

Choosing a bank

Banks do tend to have something of a hold over you; it's called security. This naturally makes it easy to criticize banks in general and for relationships to become adversarial. Remember though that it takes two to tango and if you've signed your house away to cover the loan, well it's your fault not their's. Hermann Hauser, who founded Acorn computers and now runs a venture capital firm, described someone who signs a bank guarantee as 'a fool with a pen'. In other words only sign when you're sure there's no other way.

Not all banks are the same. Here's a checklist to help you choose, or review your current bank.

- **Location** – is your bank manager in the next town or the next county? You want someone who understands your local economy.

- **Accessible** – internet banking is a must nowadays; it's just so convenient. How good is your bank online?

- **Interested** – you are part of a portfolio of customers. Are they all like you, or are the rest smaller businesses in a different sector? Your bank must be excited that you're a customer.

- **Flexible** – automatons with underwriting software on their laptop do not make good bank managers, but some are like that. Seek a relationship.

- **Glamorous** – paying through the nose for an exclusive, prestige bank's cheques with which to pay the bills might not be your best investment.

GEORGE

An entrepreneur with a small portfolio of small businesses under his wing, George enjoys a good working relationship with his bank manager Sharon. They usually meet to talk over lunch in a coffee shop close to her office. While George does not borrow money himself, the businesses he works with often do.

Sharon knows that when George is involved her risk is usually lower and this reflects in her lending decisions. It suits George to have one bank working with those he invests in and introduces Sharon. Both gain by working together. This is how it should always be with your bank too.

10 things your trading terms should embrace

If you want small print for the back of your estimates and invoices, then borrow what you like from someone else's small print. Being entrepreneurial is about being upfront, not about using small print to catch out the customer. Think about these ten aspects of trading terms.

1. **Deposits** – if you're buying materials to fulfil the order, ask for some money upfront. There's nothing wrong with asking for 30% or more with the order.

2. **Pay on delivery** – why not ask for the balance on delivery? Many web designers will not post your new site on the internet until you've paid.

3. **Odd numbers** – if you ask for payment in 30 days, you'll inevitably wait until the end of the following month. Invoice for payment in 7, 14, 21 or 28 days.

4. **Retainers** – if you're working with someone on an ongoing basis, give both of you regular cashflow and charge a monthly retainer. This works well with consultancy.

5. **Service agreements** – really, these are retainers by another name. If maintenance is part of your customer offer, service agreements enable you to schedule routine service calls rather than responding only to call-outs.

6. **Discounts** – if you want early payment, make it worth the customer's while.

7. **Incentives** – if referrals are how you win new clients, offer an incentive to reward those who make introductions.

8. **Prompt payment discount** – add a standard 5% surcharge to your invoice and then show this as a discount for payment-within terms. For some reason, this confuses corporate accounts people into settling on time!

9. **Statements** – seen by many as a cop-out from chasing debts, there is no doubt that many companies pay only when they get a statement; send one in good time.

10. **Use the phone** – whatever your terms of business, there really is no better way of making sure you get paid on time; polite, pressing phoning prompts payment.

You will notice that the focus of the preceding checklist is on getting payment. Cash is the lifeblood of any business and when you are growing you simply cannot have too much of it. Too many people are afraid to ask for the money, choosing instead to send statements and grumpy letters. Here are a few phrases you might find useful when asking for the cheque:

- Your job was one of our biggest this month and your payment is important to our cash flow. Tell me, when can I expect to see the cheque?

- We had to call in a few favours from suppliers to meet your deadline and don't want to keep them waiting for their money. First though I need to ask you to pay us. Tell me, when can I expect to see the cheque?

- We're about to invest in a new xyz, which will enable us to do an even better job for you. However, I need to show our bank that we're good at getting the money in. So please, could you send me that cheque.

- Look, I'm working alongside your guys and they got paid last month; I didn't. It's really embarrassing for me. Why have you not paid me yet?

Others will tell you all sorts of gimmicky ways of chasing overdue payments. Avoid trying to be clever – be honest and open instead.

Credit cards

Do not underestimate the value of accepting credit card payments. Many young businesses use them as a line of credit so why not take payment in this way? Although you will pay a commission to your provider (merchant), you will get the money up front while your customer may have up to 60 days to pay.

10 things about overdrafts you need to know

Embedded within business folklore is the myth that every business has to have an overdraft. It is true that few can manage growth without one, but overdrafts are rather like obesity; largely self-inflicted and difficult to lose. Reflect on these ten points.

1. **Guarantee** – overdrafts are nearly always underwritten by your personal guarantee. You're paying a high interest rate to borrow your own money.

2. **Mortgage** – increasing your mortgage on your home can provide cheap money for your business. Your personal liability is no greater than if you had an overdraft.

3. **Fees** – banks charge fees to arrange overdrafts, take guarantees and anything else they can think of.

4. **Brittle** – overdrafts can be called in at any time. Too often, the bank gets windy, calls in the overdraft and you're out of the game.

5. **More debt = less profit** – in other words, if you lost the overdraft the interest charges would appear in your books as profit.

6. **Who's boss?** – however hard you try, when you've a large overdraft you feel beholden to the bank manager, who then becomes your manager calling the shots.

7. **Reports** – most banks demand monthly management accounts when you're in the red. This is good practice, but really the figures should be for you, not someone else. It's your business, remember?

8. **Boing!** – one of the most damaging things any business can do is issue a cheque that bounces. It wrecks relationships and poses a constant risk if you live near the limit.

9. **Time** – with an overdraft, you have less time. Your cash flow is tight and delays, cock-ups and all the human things that happen cost you time you cannot afford.

10. **Insurance** – many banks sell you insurance so that the overdraft is repaid if you die or get very sick. This insurance is surprisingly expensive; it's another one of those unexpected costs.

Of course, overdrafts are not all bad news and most of us have them from time to time. The art is not thinking of an overdraft as being essential, especially when you start your business. Too many people use their overdraft to pay themselves a salary when, frankly, they'd be better living more frugally and leaving the money in the bank. Overdrafts should be used to:

- provide working capital for the everyday trading you do;
- give you a little flexibility to cope with the unexpected.

Some of our case study businesses found ways to start their business without an overdraft:

- Malcolm used contract labour and worked alongside them at night to reduce costs;
- Simon worked as a postman every morning, starting in his own office at 10am;
- Raymond drove a lorry, doing business via his mobile phone along the way.

10 loans and how to raise them

Overdrafts then are not for the long term. You could seek a business angel or you could borrow the money. Here are ten places you could look.

1. **Credit cards** – people starting consultancy or design businesses always seem the most skilled at moving debt around their credit cards, taking advantage of interest free introductory offers.

2. **Bank loan** – always secured against your assets, but with planned repayments. Unlike an overdraft, a loan cannot be called in.

3. **Prince's Trust** – if you're under 30 and starting out, this trust might lend you money when everyone else says no. The trust also finds you a business mentor.

4. **Old policies** – check out those long-term insurance policies you fund. You might be able to borrow against them at a low interest rate.

5. **Mortgage** – release some equity from the family home. It's cheap, but often unsettling for those you love and live with. Be sure to pay it back!

6. **Small firms loan guarantee scheme** – if you have not got the assets to secure a bank loan, sometimes you can get one of these. The loan is underwritten by the Government who give the bank 85% of the cash if your business fails.

7. **Sell and lease back** – you can usually sell and lease back business assets such as machinery and vehicles; this frees up cash, rather like a loan.

8. **Factoring** – by putting your debtors with a factor, who pays you straight away for a fee and then collects your debts, you gain almost one month's turnover straight away.

9. **Public sector** – councils and the many quangos that exist to drive economic regeneration often offer loan schemes. Check them out.

10. **Make sure** – before burdening your business with debt make sure that it really is necessary. Work out how you'd get there without the loan. Is this a better route for you to take?

Borrowing money has to be good for you and your business. Almost inevitably, profit as a percentage of turnover falls as your business grows. The total profit you hope will increase, but operational efficiency and processes need to become slicker in the bigger organization.

Growth for growth's sake is rather pointless, unless you want to build your business to sell, or plan to salt away enough to retire to a life of luxury. Of the businesses created in the UK each year, only a few will:

- grow to exceed £1m in turnover;
- be sold for enough money for their owners to buy a large yacht;
- 'run themselves' so that you can enjoy the salaried freedom you might be dreaming about.

However, statistically, if you start a business it is more likely to make you a multimillionaire than the lottery or any other bet you might place. With your own business you are gambling on yourself, not chance.

Arranging bank loans

Too many people use overdraft finance to cover longer term debt. Overdrafts are really funding cash flow and you should seek a loan to cover your longer term business funding needs. You could seek a business angel, or you could borrow the money. Here are ten places you could look:

- Have your business plan up to date.
- Project your cash flow with and without the investment.
- Show your bank an optimistic and a pessimistic forecast.
- Have a 'get out route' if the investment doesn't work.
- Show how others have profited from doing what you're planning to do.

10 ways to deal with running out of cash

Growing businesses often run out of cash. It's one of the major causes of business collapse. Quite simply, as turnover grows so does demand for working capital. Here are ten things to watch out for to avoid this happening to you.

1. **See it coming** – if you use a spreadsheet to forecast your cash flow accurately, you will see the danger signs a few months in advance.

2. **Chase your debts** – if you are busy, getting paid often slips down the priority list. Chase your debts and get the cash in.

3. **Stall suppliers** – everyone does this when things get tight. However, clever people discuss the issue with their supplier first then they're less likely to worry.

4. **Plot the course** – again, use a spreadsheet to work out the depth and length of your crisis. Make a plan and stick to it.

5. **Tell the bank** – as long as you have a plan and can show that you're on top of the situation, the bank will often provide short-term additional finance.

6. **Shift stock** – look around and see if you're carrying stock you could quickly liquidate. Sell the stuff you no longer need.

7. **Salary holiday** – stopping your own pay for a month or so shows those around you that you are committed to winning. When things are fixed take a bonus!

8. **VAT** – talk to those you pay tax to and explain the situation. They'll often negotiate a deferred payment deal to help you out.

9. **Pre-payments** – watch out that you're not using pre-payments for future work to pay for supplies used to meet today's orders. This might indicate that you're insolvent.

10. **Get tough** – you need to squeeze money back into your cash flow. Maybe there are things you could actually do without? Batten down the hatches and chuck excess expense overboard.

Banks will tell you that when cash gets tight it's because the business owner:

- has no proper cash flow forecast so is caught out when it's almost too late;

- takes it personally and goes into denial ignoring the risk and getting angry;
- blames others and fails to recognize the need to change the way they operate;
- panics and becomes less efficient risking customer and supplier goodwill;
- gives up the fight before they've even started.

The art is to see danger coming and trim your business to weather the storm. You need to prepare a cash flow forecast that allows you to see the impact on your overdraft of sharp increases in sales, delays in customer payments and rises in your business costs. Many business support organizations and banks can give you prepared spreadsheets into which you simply enter your own figures. These are great – they also form a prompt list for the things you might otherwise overlook. People often forget to include in their cash flow forecasting:

- VAT payments, due quarterly;
- VAT collected on sales;
- employer's national insurance;
- quarterly payments, for example machinery leases;
- repayments of existing loans.

11 Bills

how to avoid bad debts and pay suppliers

10 things all good customers have in common

It may seem obvious, but there is more to a good customer than initially meets the eye. Here then, are ten traits which combine to make the perfect customer.

1. **Trust** – the best thing customers can give you is their trust. In return, you must be honest and trust them too. If they pay without quibble, your invoicing must be scrupulously fair.

2. **Tolerance** – a sure sign of a good trading relationship is where problems are resolved amicably. Tolerance is about taking the long term view; it is not about conflict.

3. **Potential** – a business that is growing can give you lots more; you will literally grow together.

4. **Status** – if you work with the best, you will be considered the best. If you work with losers, your life will be marked by bumps and struggles.

5. **Friends** – the well-networked business will pass you around. Clearly, you'll be steered away from direct competitors but you will be introduced to friends.

6. **Good address** – customers from good neighbourhoods will often buy more from you. They are also likely to give you high quality referrals.

7. **Vision** – if your customers know where they are going, they define your role in their future. You can work together to develop new ideas. You can win long-term contracts.

8. **Faults** – when you see customers' faults, you've really got to know them well. If you can fix faults without being asked, you are indispensable.

9. **Fun** – Plato said you could learn more from an hour's play than a year's conversation. Have fun with your customers. Play to win!

10. **Cash** – it may seem obvious, but some really nice firms lead their marketplace but run on fresh air. However good a business, it can only help you if fully funded.

Finding customers itself could be the subject of a book; guides to sales and marketing abound. Here, distilled to around 120 words, is the very essence of how to find and sell to customers:

- know what you are selling and what about it will appeal most;
- find out where your customers are and what they do/read/listen to;
- make your marketplace aware of your offer by making news;
- if people buy what you have from distributors, find distributors;
- if people buy direct, go out and knock on some doors;
- create opportunities to talk to people able to buy who have the authority to buy;
- listen, question and understand what your prospects are looking for and why;
- demonstrate how you are the answer they are looking for;
- gain their commitment. Offer alternatives so that it's difficult to say no.;
- deliver what you've promised, then ask to be referred to their contacts.

You will be better at selling if you:

- are yourself and do not pretend to be what you are not;
- are honest and tell it like it is;
- listen more than you talk;
- smile;
- keep your word and do what you promise;
- never knock the competition;
- always talk about benefits, rather than the features of your product or service;
- ask for the business and wait . . . for an answer;
- control the flow of conversation without interrupting;
- never offer or accept bribes.

10 things all good suppliers have in common

Your suppliers are as important to you as your customers. This is true if you are a manufacturer buying components or a consultancy with freelance associates. Your best suppliers will be those that offer you these ten qualities.

1. **Trust** – as with customers, trust is the most important thing to have. Your reputation hangs on your suppliers' ability to meet your needs.

2. **Tolerance** – you are going to get caught out and also make mistakes. Good suppliers anticipate your need and tolerate your 'off moments'.

3. **Potential** – you want suppliers who can grow with you. They should share your ambition and be prepared to invest in keeping up with you.

4. **Quality** – wherever possible you need to buy the best. Don't encourage suppliers to cut corners to reduce costs. You will be the loser.

5. **Stability** – bickering and shareholder feuds can screw up any business. If your supplier is unstable, it could rock your boat too.

6. **Good suppliers** – your supplier buys as well as sells. How good are their suppliers?

7. **Deep pockets** – when your cash flow hiccups, the first people you lean on for credit are your suppliers. Can they support you in times of trouble?

8. **Great people** – any business is only as good as its people. Good suppliers have motivated, able, enthusiastic people.

9. **Enquiring minds** – nothing stays the same for long. You want suppliers that are constantly seeking improvement.

10. **Fun** – you will get more from your suppliers if their people play with your people. Why not challenge them to five-a-side football?

Finding good suppliers is as important as finding good customers. In fact, to enjoy success you need both. Here are some places you might look:

- trade journals;
- industry exhibitions;
- local business networks;

- the internet;
- competitors' products (to identify component suppliers);
- professional organizations (to identify associates);
- neighbours, for recommendations;
- foreign trade missions able to introduce overseas suppliers;
- university research teams working in your area;
- newspapers reporting business achievement.

You will be a better customer to your suppliers if you:

- agree annual targets and work together to achieve them;
- confirm orders in writing and make them clear and specific;
- don't blame your suppliers for your own mistakes;
- pay when you say you will, even if it's late;
- give constructive feedback to encourage innovation

JULIAN and his brother Lincoln are printers. Their firm was established by their great-grandfather and they are very much part of their local business scene. Not content to rest on the laurels of previous generations, they have invested substantially in premises, plant and people.

Julian is never complacent about his role as a supplier. His quotations are delivered quickly, the customer always knows where their job is in the production process and he watches his rivals all the time.

Keen on water sports, Julian invested in equipment for his speedboat that enables even novice water-skiers to succeed. Most summer weekends he is out with customers teaching them a new skill and building the bond of trust between them.

10 ways to ask for overdue payment

Getting the money in is vital. Sometimes you need to chase overdue payments. Here are ten ways to get the cash in.

1. **Ask** – obvious though it sounds, many people are reluctant to ask for money, choosing instead to write or send statements. Always ask.

2. **Statements** – some companies only pay when a statement arrives.

3. **Know** – who raises the payments in each of your customer's companies. Treat them as equals and take an interest in their lives. Ask to be put on the next pay run.

4. **Pop-in** – calling for a cheque is sometimes embarrassing but often works. This works best with consumers.

5. **Ring at home** – Companies House can tell you where directors live. A phone call in the evening can sometimes get you talking to the person who matters, but who is inaccessible during the day.

6. **Solicitors** – many law firms offer a debt-chasing service. Use as a last resort.

7. **Factor** – factoring your invoices means the factor pays you and then chases the customer. This is not an opportunity to deal with risky customers!

8. **Small claim** – it is a simple, but lengthy process to take a customer to the small claims court. You can do it yourself but it does take time.

9. **Garnishee order** – if the customer's going bust, getting a garnishee order from the court means you get paid directly by their customers. Great if what you sold has been sold on.

10. **Why bother?** – it's the small debts that always annoy. Every month they take time, cause anxiety and simply sit on your books. Write off small bad debts and move on.

Managing customer expectations is the key to getting paid. Equally important is remaining objective and not reacting emotionally when things go wrong. If you are a regular supplier you will be talking to your customer all the time. In this case chatting through the invoices yet to be paid should form part of your everyday conversation.

If you sell one-off products or services you need to spell out to the customer what your trading terms are. This is best done when the order is placed and confirmed.

When asking for payment:

- Be accurate and have the figures to hand;
- remain polite, never lose your temper;
- if there's a problem with your product or service, apologize and fix it;
- listen to the reasons offered;
- be sympathetic if the reason for delay is genuine.

ARTHUR had a courier business and he asked a design company he worked for to produce a company brochure for him. He wanted the brochure because business was difficult. He could not pay for the work done and shared his business problems with his customer.

The design company happened to do work for a mortgage broker who helped Arthur remortgage his house to inject more capital into his business. The brochure and extra cash gave Arthur's business the momentum it needed. He now employs 15 people.

Sometimes you have to be very creative when collecting overdue debts.

10 ways to win the order

Selling cannot be dealt with in just a few words. It is the energy that fires your business growth. Everyone has to be able to sell. Here are ten ways to become better at winning orders.

1. **Buy** – reflect on what it is that makes *you* buy. What do you like salespeople to say to you? Do they show genuine interest? Learn by buying. (But don't spend too much!)

2. **Read** – there are many good books on sales technique. Read one, but do not inhibit your natural style or personality.

3. **Listen** – people usually want to buy otherwise they wouldn't give you their time. Ask them what they want from you. Let them do the thinking.

4. **Know** – your rivals' products or services inside out. Never knock them; simply focus on the differences that support your case.

5. **Persist** – sometimes big decisions take a lot of making. Don't give up along the way.

6. **Care** – think of your prospects as human beings and not orders waiting to be placed. Show that your interest is genuine and from the heart.

7. **Reassure** – build confidence in you and what you are selling.

8. **Illustrate** – pictures can say more than words.

9. **Visit** – encourage your prospects to meet existing customers. Make the introduction, and then let them talk about you when you're not there.

10. **Believe** – if you are passionate that you are offering the best option to your customers, you will succeed. If you're only after the cash it'll be much harder.

You don't necessarily have to be well-versed in the stages of the sale to succeed at selling. Sometimes the so-called professional salesperson comes over as being just a little too glib to be totally believable. In fact some of the most successful salespeople don't conform at all. Instead they win business through determination, character and, sometimes, even cheek!

A good way to think about how you are going to sell is to consider the reasons why people buy. A good mnemonic to help you remember is the word SPACED. Each letter represents a common reason for buying – what salespeople call a buying motive:

Security – is this safe and will it work?
Performance – will it meet my needs?
Appearance – does it look good?
Convenience – is it easy to introduce and use, or will it disrupt?
Economical – can I afford to run it? How much will it save me?
Durability – will it last long enough for me to recoup the investment?

JAMIE is sales manager for a firm that supplies photocopiers and printers. His marketplace has changed dramatically over the past few years. To really benefit from the machines he sells, his customers need to learn to use their copier as a network printer. However, human nature being what it is, people are reluctant to let go of their trusty old laser printers to embrace the latest technology.

To make it easy for people to see the cost saving, Jamie provides a spreadsheet that allows them to work out what they are currently paying for printing and compare this cost with that of the new technology. The figures they calculate usually makes Jamie's solution look good value.

Jamie works hard to sell the value of working out the cost of printing. His customers then sell themselves the idea that a new copier will save them money.

10 ways to network

Meeting the right people to do business with is a challenge in itself. Everybody knows that networking delivers better results than cold calls. Here are ten networking tips to help you meet more of the right people.

1. **Carry cards** – never go anywhere without your business cards. Make sure your card clearly says what it is you do.

2. **Join things** – it almost doesn't matter what you join, as long as it's an organization where the people you want to meet tend to congregate.

3. **Volunteer** – whatever you join, become active. Become a committee member; create opportunities for people to need to talk to you.

4. **Ask questions** – when you attend business events, make sure you're one of the first to ask the speaker a good question; it gets you noticed.

5. **Look the part** – dress to look successful in your field. You do not have to wear a grey suit. Women have more scope; use it!

6. **Wear a badge** – most networking events kit you out with a name badge. Why not have your own badge made? It makes you more noticeable and easier to approach.

7. **Shake hands** – always greet people with a smile and a firm, but not too tight a handshake. Look them in the eye as you say 'hello'; you'll appear confident.

8. **Listen** – the art of networking is to encourage the person you're meeting to share their views, hopes, needs and wants. Talk about them, not you.

9. **Move on** – don't spend the entire event with one person. To move on without seeming rude, hold their arm as you make your excuse to move; for some reason this always makes it seem OK.

10. **Take notes** – take a moment to record what you've said, heard or promised to do; otherwise you'll have forgotten by tomorrow morning.

Networking is rather like a bank savings account – you have to make several deposits before you can hope to earn interest and make a withdrawal. There are several business networking clubs you might consider joining. Some are specific to an area or industry, others form part of national and international networks. For example, if you joined the local branch of one of the large breakfast networking organizations you would probably find:

- up to 50 people who meet on the same morning every week;
- no direct competitors as most limit membership to one per business sector;
- an opportunity to talk every week about what you're looking for;
- regular opportunities to talk to the group about what you do;
- networking training sessions;
- members committed to introducing each other to new customers.

Online networks provide an almost overwhelming array of people you can network with. Most have a search facility to enable you to identify common interests and various forums where you can debate pertinent issues.

In some cities, you will also find professional networking facilitators. These are individuals or firms who arrange events at which people can meet each other. These are rather like dating agencies in the way that they work, except business is the objective rather than pleasure.

MAX

A strategic marketer with a lot of small business experience, Max is an active member of the Ecademy internet-based business network (*www.ecademy.com*). He focuses on helping people position their business offer so that others can see the benefits more clearly. He freely gives his time and expertise to help those he meets.

By investing in others he has created a network of people who know that his advice works, for they have benefited from it themselves. They introduce other people to Max when they need help with their marketing. Max makes his living from those he meets in this way.

12 Home

premises – the why/where/how/
how not

10 good reasons to work from home

Technology means that you can appear to be wherever you wish. You can, quite literally, conduct your business from the beach. More realistic perhaps is to control your overhead costs by working from home. Here are ten good reasons for doing this.

1. **Cheap** – the money you save by not renting an office can be invested instead in technology, marketing and other things that build your business.

2. **Commuting** – travelling a few feet to the office each day can make a refreshing change after years of catching the 07:30 train. Work longer hours in shorter days.

3. **Convenient** – if you are the creative type, or just like to work at odd times, working from home means you can go into the office whenever you want.

4. **Childcare** – while something of a two-edged sword, working from home makes childcare a lot easier. It's also easier to fit your work around school sports day!

5. **Coffee shops** – even those with an office frequently choose to meet clients in a mutually convenient coffee shop. You have no excuse for not drinking lots of latte!

6. **Crises** – life is littered with domestic crises. You can minimize the impact of many of them by being around when the plumber decides to answer your call.

7. **Comfortable** – OK, you need to create a work-like environment, but when you're having a day at the office you can dress down as far as you like.

8. **Colleagues** – you will undoubtedly have people who work with you either regularly or on a project basis. Working from home means you have to plan meetings with the result that they should be more focused and effective.

9. **Classical?** – if you like to listen to music, you can. You also avoid the debate about windows open or closed; you create your own environment.

10. **Colds** – you know when someone starts sneezing in an open plan office? Soon everyone's reaching for the tissues. Working from home is healthy too!

Some people, however, really do need the discipline of working alongside others. If this is you, then consider:

- **Sharing** – a rented office with someone else. You don't have to be working in the same business, just someone like you who wants a work buddy.

- **Hot desk** – many business centres now provide hot-desking. This enables you to work with others around you. Some people need a work environment for work.

- **Empty office?** – ask your customers, suppliers, friends and neighbours. Often people are happy to let an unused office be occupied by someone they know.

- **Clubs** – particularly in London, there are many clubs and organizations that provide their members with places to meet, work and do business.

- **The park** – be creative in deciding on your workspace. Wireless technology means you can now work online from anywhere; why not write your next proposal in the park?

If you do work from home you must remember:

- to make sure you have office contents and public liability insurance;

- that you can reclaim some of the household bills against your profits;

- that it makes sense to tell your neighbours if you're going to have lots of visitors;

- your workspace should not be exclusively for your business – this can have tax repercussions;

- to have a separate work phone number so that you can answer it professionally.

Workshops

If you need storage or space to make things, all of the above points also apply to you. It's just that you need a bigger space with easy access and perhaps a three-phase power supply. Often, it is easier to find workshop space than office space.

10 ways to look bigger than you are

Sometimes, small is beautiful. However, when you're pitching for really big contracts it often pays to look bigger than you are. This avoids the worry that you will not be able to deliver. Here are ten ways to look bigger.

1. **Good address** – if you work from home, adapt your address to make it look more like a business address. Avoid PO Box numbers; they can make you look shady.

2. **Phone answering** – have your phone diverted to a call answering service when you are out.

3. **Share facilities** – if you share a building with someone who's got a better meeting room than you, share it when important clients visit.

4. **Website** – your virtual business environment should always be a few steps ahead of reality. Websites are cheaper than premises and are usually visited more often.

5. **Nice car** – however hard we try not to, we all judge our visitors by the cars they drive. If you usually go to your customers, make sure you drive a nice car. Also keep it clean!

6. **Think big** – your words will give you away. Make sure you think, talk and walk big. Remember, anything is possible if you want it badly enough.

7. **Associates** – a network of associates gives you manpower when you need it, and no overhead costs when you don't.

8. **Branding** – if subcontractors visit your customers, perhaps as service engineers or to make deliveries, have your mark on their vehicles.

9. **Proactive** – big businesses usually appear to be efficient. Investing in client management software and regularly mailing your prospects create that successful, large image.

10. **Bluff** – in reality big firms can be less efficient than small ones. The art is to say 'yes, no problem' to the customer, then sort out how to deliver later!

Often, the need to appear larger than you are, or perhaps be based in more prestigious premises, is more your worry than your customers'. Remember that most companies in the UK are small, employing fewer than five people. If you need reassuring that it's good to be small, here are some benefits to consider.

- **Low overheads** – small businesses have small overheads and usually provide better value.

- **Best people** – too often, the person who impresses you when the deal is done is not the person who does the work. With small firms 'what you see is what you get'.

- **Adaptable** – unrestrained by inflexible systems and tradition, small firms are usually happy to adapt to deliver exactly what you want.

- **Accountable** – small firms cannot pass you round the houses, each person passing the buck. Small firms take responsibility for what they do.

- **Transparent** – large corporates can often seem anonymous and it's actually hard to see who or what is behind the façade. Small businesses rarely have secrets.

MICHELLE

Wanting to combine a love of cooking with raising two children, Michelle started a catering business based in her kitchen at home. The business grew, and so did the children. Now they are at school she has moved her business to a local golf club. Here she has more space and a captive market for her food. Michelle's business location has changed as her needs have changed. She is taking her business where she wants to go.

10 premises traps and how to avoid them

If your business is growing it will inevitably need premises. Unless you are able to buy a place you will need to rent or lease premises. Here are ten things to look out for.

1. **Long lease** – most leases are short these days. You want to be able to move on if you outgrow the place; it's usually best to avoid long leases.

2. **Break clauses** – good leases have break clauses; these are opportunities to 'break' the lease and move out.

3. **Repairs** – check if you are to be liable for repairs; repairs can be expensive!

4. **Rates** – it's easy to forget that you'll also be paying local authority business rates. These can be high, particularly for retail premises.

5. **Service charge** – if you're in a shared complex, you will probably be asked to pay a service charge. Will you need all that this provides you with?

6. **Power** – many landlords individually meter and mark-up electricity, gas and telephony. Compare the rates with what you pay now; how much more will it be costing you?

7. **Neighbours** – what your neighbours do will make a difference. It's difficult to run a call centre, for example, with a foundry in the next unit.

8. **Restrictions** – sometimes your lease or agreement will exclude some activities you might want to carry out. Check carefully.

9. **Security** – insuring your enterprise in business premises can be expensive. For one thing, there's usually no one there at night. For another, in a shared building you cannot always be sure that others will lock the door.

10. **Parking** – your staff might all come to work by bus, but if your customers drive to you where will they park? See how busy the car park gets before you sign.

Most landlords use a standard lease that is simply adapted for each unit. Leases are legal documents and there is often a court fee payable when it is set up. This is to protect the landlord from you claiming security of tenure over and above the terms you have agreed in the lease. It is always wise to take independent legal advice before signing a lease for premises.

A place of your own

While it is often prudent to rent business premises and focus your own investment on the operational side of your venture, buying a place of your own makes sense in some circumstances. What's more, buying premises can be easier than you might think. It is possible, in some circumstances, for the owners of a business to pool their pension funds and use this as the deposit for a commercial property with the remainder being covered by a commercial mortgage. The mortgage payments are funded from the monthly rent you pay. When you retire, the property is sold to provide a tax-free lump sum to purchase annuities for the owner. Pension legislation is complex and frequently changing so take independent advice. However, the principle of using the rent you would otherwise pay to a landlord to fund your pension is worth considering, particularly if you expect to remain at the same location for many years.

Redundant buildings

To encourage you to restore a derelict building, grants are often available to contribute to the capital costs. Finding the right place can give you the chance to develop the buildings as your business grows, funding the development from cash flow.

> GEORGE purchased a derelict farmhouse and buildings. A grant helped with the conversion costs and because he was going to live there too he obtained a homeowner's mortgage, which costs less than a commercial loan. His company pays him rent for the space it occupies and this more than covers the mortgage.

10 things about franchises you might not know

Franchising is a great way to do business. For the franchisor it enables rapid growth with less debt. For franchisees there's a proven business model to follow. Here are ten things you might not know.

1. **It's big** – there are almost 700 franchisors operating in the UK. There's a franchise business to suit almost everyone's interest and expertise.

2. **It's everywhere** – franchising is not just about fast food and instant print; check out *www.british-franchise.org* and be surprised!

3. **It works** – almost all franchisors are successful and profitable. They have a trade body and code of practice to protect franchisees.

4. **It can work for you too** – although, on average, franchisees pay their franchisor 8% of their turnover, this is in effect an investment. Most of the potentially expensive pitfalls have been signposted so that you avoid them.

5. **They sometimes say no** – if a franchisor doesn't think you're cut out for life in their business, they'll tell you.

6. **Exclusivity** – you usually buy an exclusive territory that holds enough prospective customers to sustain your successful business.

7. **Friends** – much of the loneliness of self-employment is banished. You are joining a network of other people, all facing the same issues and not competing with each other and so able to share.

8. **Banks** – because they know your chances of success are high, banks are often happier to lend you the money to take on a franchise.

9. **National deals** – by providing a national network of local providers, franchisors can negotiate deals, on behalf of their franchisees, with major corporate customers needing nationwide access to services.

10. **It might not be you** – taking a franchise means following rules. It is only by doing what others have proved works that you will succeed with a franchise. Franchising is not about 'doing your own thing'.

If you are looking to grow your business, then setting up franchisees is not necessarily an easy option. The cynical view that you can grow your business with others bearing the risk is not strictly true. Before seeking franchisees you have to demonstrate that your business model will replicate. The best way to do this is to open an outlet from scratch that follows what you see as the winning formula. Carefully documenting how this outlet grows forms the basis for your offer to potential franchisees.

Franchisees are often people who have:

- left corporate life and want to work for themselves;
- relevant skills but lack the ability or desire to 'reinvent the wheel';
- money to invest, often a redundancy cheque;
- passion and determination.

Franchising does not suit people who are:

- strongly individualistic;
- not comfortable managing money and people;
- focused on their own way of doing things;
- unable to commit their all to a new venture.

MARK & DIANE

Following high-flying careers as helicopter pilot and airline purser, Mark and Diane wanted to work for themselves. Mark's RAF pension gave them money to live on while they established a business, but they were not sure what they wanted to do.

They decided to open a pine retail store and joined a franchise network. The franchisor's assistance with finding premises, securing a lease, merchandizing and launching the showroom was invaluable. Mark says, 'The store opening team arrived from Head Office well in time for my launch day and stayed with us until I found my feet.'

For Mark and Diane, franchising provided a ready made solution. Their shop in North Wales is successful and trade is growing. Buying a franchise has helped them realize a dream.

13 People

recruiting without fears of future tears

10 questions to ask when recruiting

Without good people your business cannot grow. Recruiting the right people is vital to your continued success. Here are ten questions you might like to ask potential recruits when interviewing.

1. **Talk me through your career to date** – make sure you explore any gaps.

2. **What has been your greatest achievement?** – find out the highlights and what they are proudest of having done.

3. **What has been your biggest mistake?** – making mistakes is how we all learn so the more the better, within reason! If they've made none they're either too cautious or fibbing.

4. **How do you want to be spending your time in three years time?** – reveal where they see their career going.

5. **What appeals most about working here?** – check out how much they've thought about what you are looking for.

6. **What appeals least about working here?** – do they trust you enough to tell you? If not, have you failed to make them feel at ease with you?

7. **If you won £1m tomorrow, how would you spend it?** – this gives you an insight into vision, aspiration and self-esteem.

8. **What is the question you would most like me to ask you?** – they might say, 'will you accept the job?' or ask something which reveals their vision for your organization.

9. **What is the question you hope I don't ask?** – again, this encourages them to reveal fears and doubts. Respect them for what they are and reassure them.

10. **When I'm making my decision, what is the single thing you want me to remember about you?** – encourages them to summarize the key benefits they bring.

Before you seek people to interview:

- define the job and write out what it will entail;
- check out the terms other employers offer for the same job;

- work out how much the new staff will cost you;
- work out how much they will make you and how long it will take to happen.

You can find new employees by:

- advertising in local, national or trade publications;
- putting a sign outside your door;
- asking existing employees who they know;
- asking customers who they know;
- networking;
- using a recruitment agency.

Job advertisements should always contain:

- the job title;
- the salary range and benefits;
- your contact details;
- a promise of confidentiality;
- positive reasons for joining your firm.

When interviewing:

- do not face the candidate over a desk – create a friendly environment instead;
- listen more than you talk;
- take notes;
- smile;
- offer to reimburse travel expenses;
- say thank you and ask for feedback on the interview.

10 ways to deal with red tape

We all hear horror stories about employment legislation. Here are ten ways to avoid getting tangled in red tape.

1. **Be nice** – 99.99% of people are decent, honest and reliable. Treat your people well and they will return the compliment by giving you their commitment.

2. **Give a contract** – get a solicitor to draft an employment contract that protects both you and your staff. Encourage the use of friendly language.

3. **Read the press** – quality newspapers usually report new or planned employment legislation. Have a view before your people ask you.

4. **Train** – invest in training so that people can do their job confidently.

5. **Listen** – create opportunities or procedures so that your people can tell you their grievances. If they tell others but not you, trouble may be looming.

6. **Comply** – make sure that your workplace is safe, comfortable and clean. Do not try to cut corners as this usually costs, rather than saves, money.

7. **Consult** – these days regulators are usually more interested in preventing problems than in prosecuting those who err. Invite them in and follow their advice.

8. **Join a club** – many business networks, for example the Chamber of Commerce and the Federation of Small Businesses, provide help and advice on red tape issues. ACAS also has a free helpline you can call. Use them.

9. **Benchmark** – find out how others deal with red tape and see if you can share information and resources. You don't need to do it all yourself.

10. **Perspective** – because it is usually imposed, red tape often seems a bigger issue than it really is. Keep it in perspective.

Actually, keeping it in perspective is very important. When you start to employ people, your business changes however much you think it will not. You are in business because you are passionate about what you do and want the freedom and control that only entrepreneurship can deliver. Employees are usually employees because they do not want to take big risks, and they enjoy the security of a regular pay cheque. Your motives for working together are different and that is what makes the difference!

What is reasonable in the workplace?

In your darker moments you will feel that the law is biased towards the employee and that red tape and legislation are converting your business into a meal ticket for those who work for you. Remember that journalists like to write about extremes, and actually common sense and pragmatism usually mean that reality rarely matches what you might fear. There are some areas, however, where you do need to tread carefully. This means making sure that you understand the law and how it applies to you. Laws often change, but here are some key areas where people often come unstuck.

- **Disability** – you should not discriminate nor should you make access to the workplace difficult. If you employ disabled workers, you can sometimes get help towards the cost of specialist equipment.

- **Equality** – just because people do not share your ideals, views, gender or values, this does not make them the wrong people to employ; cherish diversity.

- **Making babies** – it is not advisable to ask about 'baby plans' when interviewing young women or to get rid of females simply because they are pregnant. Both can land you in deep, boiling hot water.

- **Performance** – if someone is not performing, you need to follow the correct procedures for dealing with this. Too often poor performance is a symptom of a business issue, not an employee issue.

- **Communication** – most workplace problems are the result of poor communication. You need to communicate with your workforce clearly, consistently and check their understanding.

10 things the best bosses have in common

It's almost a cliché but it can never be said too many times – your people are the biggest investment your business will ever make. For most businesses the wage bill is the biggest monthly cost. Here are ten ways you can become a better boss.

1. **Big ears** – good bosses not only listen, they take a genuine interest in their staff.

2. **Long legs** – be seen to be interested and involved; walk around the place, visit customers.

3. **White teeth** – smiling bosses make people happy. If the problem is not one your staff can help you solve, keep it to yourself.

4. **Dirty hands** – in most small businesses, there are always grotty jobs like unblocking toilets. If you lead from the front others will follow.

5. **An open door** – at times you need to be left alone and not everything you do can be shared, but being accessible is the best way to know what's happening.

6. **Good vision** – people only follow leaders who know where they're going.

7. **Tongue control** – emotional responses, such as shouting and ranting, have their place but not if it means humiliating your staff. Sometimes it's best to hold your tongue.

8. **Strong stomach** – remember how officers led their men to certain death in the battles of the Somme? Like them, you must not let your fears show.

9. **Firm hand** – you are the boss. You are expected to make unpopular decisions where necessary and to be firm with those who don't pull their weight.

10. **Love** – we are all human. We all like to be loved; good bosses show true love and compassion. Being heartless and brutal will not make you rich.

It may sound idealistic to be a touchy-feely caring employer when the bank has a charge over your house and things aren't going as well as you'd hoped. However, being a great boss need not cost you the Earth. Here are a few very affordable ways to make your business a great place to work.

- **Soft loo paper** – pay the extra few pence for the good stuff. Also make sure toilets are clean and in good working order.

- **Graffiti board** – why not create places for your staff to have their say, free from criticism or retribution?

- **Good tools** – usually the best tools cost less than the wrong tools and waste less time.

- **Party** – investing £10 per head in a visit to the pub after work on Friday can deliver hundreds of pounds worth of extra work next week.

- **Surprises** – we all like nice surprises, for example ice cream on a hot day.

CLIVE

When Clive took over a company he had once worked for, he was determined to be a better employer than his boss had been. When he'd worked there before, cash had been tight and improvisation part of everyday life.

Although he reorganized the workshops improving the workflow and buying new equipment, one of the most popular improvements was the £70 microwave oven installed in the freshly painted staffroom.

10 ways to delegate and share the burden

Letting go of the stuff you used to do is the only way to grow your business. As headcount rises, your job becomes more strategic with others doing the day-to-day tasks. Here are ten tips on delegation.

1. **Make it clear** – explain what you want done and why.

2. **Train** – invest time in showing people how to do it.

3. **Encourage innovation** – accept that others might find better ways than yours to get things done.

4. **Don't blame** – it won't always be right first time. Encourage and nurture, rather than rant and rave.

5. **Allow routine** – let operational things become a series of routines. You might prefer every day to be an adventure, your staff probably would not.

6. **Empower** – make people responsible for their actions and give them scope to be flexible and to adapt.

7. **Don't interfere** – having delegated, the worst thing you can do is interfere. Wait to be asked for help. Make sure that deadlines are being met though.

8. **Make a list** – what is on your desk for this week? Separate what needs you and what can be delegated. Now delegate some of the things you think only you can do. Allow your people to surprise you!

9. **Explore new things** – if you can delegate all your tasks you are not redundant. You now have time to build your business's future.

10. **Review** – reviewing what has been done and helping everyone strive for improvement will encourage you to keep delegating.

Guilt

One of the things no one tells you about is the feeling of guilt that often accompanies success and business growth. Your innate modesty might well make you attribute your success thus far to good fortune. Moving away from the coalface and letting others do what you have come to know as work may then feel difficult. Here are a few thoughts to help you through this moment:

- only you have the track record to do the strategic stuff;

- most people relish routine and security. As an employer you provide it; as an entrepreneur you look beyond it;

- people will enjoy being trusted with tasks that were recently yours;

- your success provides your employees with job security.

Getting strategic

So you've delegated and now have time on your hands. Here are five things you could do tomorrow that you didn't have time to consider today:

- clear your desk of clutter, put your feet up and read your business plan;

- talk to your five best customers;

- research your competitors;

- take time out, relax and think where you want your business to go;

- book a surprise weekend away and treat your family to your attention.

14 Motivation

adding momentum and magic

10 ways to manage a team

Business is booming and you've created a team. Here are ten things you need to think about if you are to keep it all together as your company grows.

1. **Business plan** – if you've been too busy to update the plan, do it now. Losing sight of the vision and strategy will make things fuzzy and hard to manage.

2. **Break it down** – create mini-business plans for each part of your business and allocate responsibility to individuals for their area's achievement.

3. **Critical paths** – mapping your business process will enable you to determine the critical path. Keep it simple or no one will understand.

4. **Writing on the wall** – put key information on the wall where everyone can see it. Make it visual; use pictures, charts and graphs rather than lots of words.

5. **Job descriptions** – make sure that everyone has agreed what their job entails. You want to avoid duplication and gaps. Remember to include the catch-all 'other duties as required' so that you can ask them to do almost anything!

6. **Appraisals** – review performance regularly. Say 'well done' and 'thank you' where appropriate. Help people to perform better.

7. **Skills** – appraisals identify skill gaps which need attention. Always review training activity afterwards and try to evaluate your return on the investment.

8. **Meetings** – we all hate endless meetings but short and snappy 'start the day' sessions can be really motivating. They also focus everyone on priorities.

9. **Communication** – as businesses grow, communication suffers. Create opportunities for formal and informal communication.

10. **Celebrate** – don't keep good news to yourself. You will only succeed because everyone's done their bit. Celebrate success together.

Management is a profession in itself. As your business grows, you will need to appoint managers. These will either be promoted from the ranks or those with the organizational skills you need will be brought in from outside.

The skills you need to be an entrepreneur and to start a business are different from those you need to manage a complex organization successfully.

Entrepreneurs	Managers
Create ideas and develop strategy	Translate strategy into action
Are rarely team players	Achieve through others
Prefer doing new things	Measure and improve performance
Just do it	Assess risks and plan to reduce them

Many entrepreneurs encounter a growth barrier when the staff totals around 15. At this point, the entrepreneurial founder has three options:

● learn to become a manager and suppress the entrepreneurial instinct;

● hire a professional manager to run the business so the owner can continue to explore;

● halt further business growth.

STEVEN & LES

Steven started his market research business from scratch. As it grew, he found himself needing to spend more and more time managing the business and less time planning the future. Les had worked in the public sector and was an excellent manager. He wanted to move to a smaller organization where he could enjoy more autonomy.

As MD of Steven's company Les has made a tremendous difference to the efficiency, focus and growth of the business. In particular, Les has introduced many new ideas which have underpinned the organization's success. Steven now spends his time working with key clients and exploring new avenues. They make a great partnership.

10 ways to make work fun for others

Management techniques will get you so far, although you want to avoid creating a stodgy, formal work environment. Whatever business you're in, some of these ten possibilities will be applicable to you.

1. **Paint the walls** – if your place is currently mucky magnolia, cover the walls in a vibrant colour; brighten up the place.

2. **Buy beanbags** – well, beanbags might be a step too far for most of us, but comfy sofas might be better for meetings than that square table and set of plastic chairs.

3. **Clean the windows** – when did the sun last shine in your workplace?

4. **Plant flowers** – if you've got space outside, plant flowers. Buy flowers to put on your desk. They will make you feel better too.

5. **Good coffee** – it's amazing how awful some cheap coffees taste. Treat people to decent drinks at work. They might want to stay longer at night!

6. **Create competitions** – light-hearted prizes for hitting key targets make winning part of your workplace culture.

7. **Organize outings** – create opportunities for colleagues and their families to play together. The closer friends they become, the more they'll gel as a team

8. **Sports** – encourage fitness by subsidizing gym membership. Challenge customers to a game of five-a-side football

9. **Fund learning** – study does something good to the mind. Helping your people develop their interests will make them more motivated at work.

10. **Volunteering** – encouraging people to volunteer for community work, perhaps using company tools and materials, will boost their self-esteem and your reputation.

Rewards packages

It really is quite simple to tailor the benefits package you offer your staff to their personal interests and needs. After all, you are probably very creative when it comes to your own pay and perks. All you have to do is make sure that:

- benefits are properly costed so that you can offer alternatives fairly;
- you provide the things the law says you should;
- people can change their benefits package as their circumstances change.

Here are a few things you might include in such a package.

- **Salary** – everyone needs money to live on.
- **Pension** – enhanced pension contributions often suit older people.
- **Car** – company cars are perks for some but penalize others.
- **Healthcare** – private healthcare for the whole family is cheaper through a company scheme than if purchased individually.
- **Life assurance** – more important for those with families than singles.
- **Other insurances** – critical illness, income replacement, etc.
- **Longer holidays** – can be traded for a lower salary.
- **Flexible hours** – opportunities to fit work around commitments like childcare.
- **Gym membership** – for individuals and perhaps even their families.
- **Homeworking** – allow people to work from home for part of the week.

As you can see, not all of these benefits cost money, and several enable you to save money on things like employer's national insurance. Your accountant should be able to advise how to widen the choice you give your employees.

10 training opportunities most overlook

Training and personal development can make a tremendous difference to the way people perform in their jobs. Don't forget that this also applies to you as the boss. However, if you thought that training had to involve spending lots of money, think again. Here are ten low cost options.

1. **Share** – if you're a small business, club together with others to organize training sessions. It usually costs a lot less than joining a course.

2. **Ask suppliers** – your suppliers gain if you become more proficient. See if they have in-house training programmes your people can attend.

3. **Teach each other** – the best training happens in the workplace with your own experts helping others catch up. Because this can happen spontaneously it's often overlooked.

4. **Work experience** – supervising students who visit you to gain work experience will develop the supervisory skills of those who do not usually manage people.

5. **School governor** – becoming a school governor provides excellent free management training. It makes people more objective in their own work.

6. **Charity trustee** – becoming a trustee enables people to develop their particular skill (for example finance, human relations or marketing) in a different context.

7. **Volunteer** – applying your skills in a new environment, away from your usual marketplace or industry, as a volunteer will broaden your ability.

8. **Quangos** – where your firm's skill needs match those recognized as barriers to national prosperity, it's often possible to get training grants from relevant quangos.

9. **Read books** – some people find it easy to learn from books; set up a company library. Include training software.

10. **Online** – the internet is packed with knowledge and abounds with the experience of others. It can also provide great learning opportunities. Look for online training providers.

Identifying training needs involves comparing the skills available within your business with your needs. Importantly, you also have to predict what future skills you will need so that people can learn ahead of demand. There's nothing worse than accepting a contract to do something you've not done before and finding that no one has the necessary skills.

Even in a small business it can be a good idea to map out the skills in your team. This is best done by creating a skills matrix, like this one for a small travel company.

	Word	Excel	Sales	French	German	Spanish
Judith	✓	✓		✓		
Michael	✓		✓			✓
Tom	✓	✓				
Ruth			✓	✓	✓	✓

It is also useful to assess the level of ability as this can identify training needs as well as experts. It also helps you match jobs to people.

You will often find, as part of this exercise, that you have skills within your team that you didn't realize you had. Even though a particular skill might have been listed on the CV when you hired someone, you may well have forgotten about it.

10 common people problems and how to solve them

Employing people can be one of the most rewarding things you do. There is an element of parenting, of teaching, of friendship and also, perhaps, of policing. This checklist might help you with some common challenges.

1. **Not performing** – talk to your staff and find out what the problem is. Problems at home can scupper performance. Don't jump to conclusions.

2. **Not reliable** – could be a sign of trouble outside the workplace. Or perhaps it's hard work getting up early in the morning!

3. **Wrong person** – we all make mistakes and hire the wrong person. Take advice before confronting and follow the correct procedures. Keep your cool.

4. **Poor health** – as long as someone is not shirking, you need to be sympathetic. Insurance can provide income after three months sickness, freeing up your cash to fund temporary help. (Insisting on medicals before hiring can reduce this risk.)

5. **Neurotic** – one in four people in the UK suffer from mental illness at some point. If you're on the receiving end of this recognize that, with professional help, many people come out of it better than before.

6. **Sex** – an awful lot of people marry someone they meet at work. Office romances, perhaps consummated in the stockroom, are part of life. Be ready with the tissues if it all goes wrong.

7. **Private calls** – don't get hung up if your people use your phone to sort out their private lives, unless it becomes excessive. Set ground rules to show what you consider reasonable.

8. **Theft** – any criminal activity should be dealt with quickly. Take advice; cover-ups and quick departures do not set a good example to others. Accept that you may be the last to know that something is going on

9. **Tragedy** – people die, become disabled, divorce, get mugged, robbed, raped and tragically attacked. Your role as employer is to listen and support. Help people when they're down and they'll help you more when they're up again.

10. **On reflection** – many people problems are symptoms of poor management. Before roaming round the workplace lopping off heads, look in the mirror and make sure you're not the problem!

Other things that can go wrong and what to do

- **Accidents at work**– if someone is injured at work you could face a heavy fine if faulty equipment or poor workplace practice was the cause. When accidents happen, sort out the emergency and then investigate fully. Cooperate with outside agencies which get involved. Be prepared to face the media.

- **Accidents somewhere else** – yes, it can be worse. Road accidents involving your vehicles, industrial accidents that pollute rivers, fires and floods all are largely avoidable but can strike. Make sure you're fully insured and have a disaster recovery plan tucked away safe.

- **Weather/war/etc.** – sometimes things happen that you cannot possibly predict or be prepared for. If the world looks like it's dealing you a rough hand, try to remain pragmatic and positive. Life's just like that sometimes.

Ways to be prepared

- **Insurance** – the remoter the risk, the lower the premium, the more devastating it can be if it happens. Get insured.

- **First aiders** – Make sure you have qualified first aiders in your team. Make sure vehicles and workplaces have first aid kits and fire extinguishers.

- **Fire drills** – practice evacuating the building regularly. Avoid this when it's raining!

- **Security** – invest in good security alarms, lights, etc.

- **Plan B** – think about the worst possible thing that could happen and think through how you would deal with it. What would life look like six months later? Make sure you arrange your life and affairs so that this apocalyptic scenario would be tolerable and you no longer have anything to fear. Life will continue, regardless.

15 Control

leading or encouraging an MBO

10 benefits to buying out your boss

Often, buying the business you work for is preferable to starting something else from scratch. Here are ten reasons to think more about this option.

1. **The devil you know** – you will get fewer surprises buying the place you work than buying something else. With an MBO you are the surprise!

2. **Unrealized potential** – you've said it for years, but no one listens. The market opportunity you can see so clearly doesn't fit the corporate vision.

3. **Overheads** – big groups spread their bloated head office costs over the operating companies. These hide the profitability you will release.

4. **Retirement** – if you work for a hands-on founder of the business, you may be the best bet. The business may not be worth much on the open market.

5. **Earn out** – the founder might be happy to help you buy the business from the profits it generates. Linking price to profit maintains interest too.

6. **New broom** – if you are popular with the team, they'll respond to your leadership and respect your investment in them. Productivity should rise.

7. **Continuity** – customers and suppliers take comfort from the stability that continuity of management means to them. They'll buy more from you.

8. **Avoids covert trading** – often, when someone leaves a business to start on their own, paranoia sets in at both camps. You cannot poach customers if instead you poach the company.

9. **Existing borrowing** – negotiating with the bank for your takeover is easier than seeking capital to set up on your own. You'll probably get away with giving less security.

10. **Running start** – the business is trading already. There's no expensive lag as you wait for activity to build in the early months.

Due diligence

You frequently hear people taking about giving 'due diligence' as part of the process of acquiring a business. All this actually means is that you need to check that you are buying what you think you are buying. It's no big deal in a small business, where your accountant can guide you through the process. For big business, it's a major exercise.

Do not underestimate the time or cost of doing due diligence checks thoroughly. After all it is your money you might be throwing away.

The other aspect of due diligence is that it should form part of the price negotiations. while it is constructive to seek a quick deal and a clean handover, your advisers may find things as part of their assessment that enable you to better the deal.

When businesses are changing hands:

- rumours spread through the workforce like wildfire;
- good people get poached by rivals;
- customers' confidence is rattled by alternative suppliers;
- senior management lose sight of operational issues as they focus on the deal;
- efficiency, morale and confidence all fall.

10 signs that a business might be on the market

One way to grow a business is to buy another and merge the two together. This can create cultural challenges when you come to do it, but it can fast track you to a bigger picture. Look out for these ten business symbols.

1. **Competitors** – who seem to be losing the plot.

2. **Rival salespeople** – who apply to you for a job.

3. **Customer feedback** – that a rival company is having a few problems.

4. **Shared customers** – who else seems to be supplying your customers?

5. **Weeds in the car park** – when businesses lose momentum routine maintenance no longer gets done.

6. **Customers migrating** – when customers leave there is usually something wrong. Your enthusiasm and focus will win them back.

7. **Court judgments** – look for firms where cash is a problem and court judgments are mounting. The owners might be facing bankruptcy and anything you can offer will be better than that!

8. **Disgruntled suppliers** – you might even be a disgruntled supplier. If order levels are falling and payments slipping this is a sure sign of trouble.

9. **Fall-outs** – when partners split, directors resign or key people leave the team you have the opportunity to rescue the survivors.

10. **They call you** – there is always the chance that someone will see you as a possible buyer and make an approach. Be receptive.

The thought of buying companies to add to your own might unleash your megalomaniac instinct. Be careful, for bigger does not necessarily mean better. If you want to grow through acquisition, choose businesses that:

- do different, but similar things to your own;

- supply products or services to your customers;

- have customers able to buy your product or service too;

- could share overhead costs to the benefit of both;

- are not too far away because you'll need to be there much of the time!

Buying a business need not cost as much as you think. It all depends on:

- the level of debt in the business (which you as buyer would take over);
- the expectations of the people selling it;
- the reason for the sale (no longer fits, wants to retire, etc.)

The money to buy a business can come from:

- your personal savings;
- the equity you have in your home(s);
- the bank;
- factoring the debtor book of the company you are buying (frees up working capital);
- liquidating dead stock and unwanted assets of the business you're buying.

Businesses come with people

Remember that businesses are usually sold with their people. Employment legislation protects employees when a firm changes hands. If someone has worked there for 20 years and are not needed in the new structure, it might fall to you to fund any redundancy payment.Organic growth is where your business simply gets bigger by itself. Often, this just happens – but the more you recognize and control it, the safer it will be. Growing too fast is a major cause of business failure. Manage the speed of growth by considering these ten factors.

10 ways to control the rate of growth

rganic growth is where your business simply gets bigger by itself. Often, this just happens – but the more you recognize and control it, the safer it will be. Growing too fast is a major cause of business failure. Manage the speed of growth by considering these ten factors.

1. **Increasing prices** – nudge up your prices as demand grows. This has the effect of shaking out the less discerning customers.

2. **Narrowing the range** – reducing the number of products or services means you can simplify systems, reduce production costs and carry less stock.

3. **Selling bits off** – aspects of the business you want to move away from might have a value to someone else. Don't just ditch what you can maybe sell.

4. **Subcontracting** – you don't have to do it all yourself. Subbing work out to others means that you don't have to build your overhead costs too quickly.

5. **Saying no** – this is the hardest thing for most entrepreneurs to do, but it is an option. You don't have to say 'yes' to every project.

6. **Taking forward orders** – scheduling your work into the distant future will enable you to make sure that as you grow the work is there. It also discourages those unwilling to wait.

7. **Upgrading your product or service** – the name of the game is to increase profit levels. Adapt your offer to add more value to the customer and more profit for you.

8. **Increasing efficiency** – usually, you can find ways of doing things more efficiently, increasing output without adding cost.

9. **Working shifts** – if you manufacture things, shift working gets more out of your equipment and space. If you sell ideas and time you might need to work over the weekend for a while.

10. **Becoming exclusive** – every business sector has its prima donnas. These are the providers everyone wants but few can afford. Successfully becoming a prima donna might mean that you needn't grow the business at all!

Rapid growth can kill a business because:

- cash flow gets squeezed and you literally run out of money;
- pressure of work reduces efficiency and increases unit cost;
- new people and plant take a while to bed in;
- mistakes are more likely;
- you get slower in raising invoices and sometimes forget.

Consultancies face special growth challenges

If you are a consultancy business, growing can present some really challenging dilemmas. The move from one overworked founder to two is a big step. Moving to a team approach, with the introduction of structure and perhaps a new approach to work, is even bigger.

When work threatens to overwhelm people selling their time and advice, things to consider include:

- hiring admin staff to do everything you cannot charge to clients;
- recruiting part-timers to carry out specific elements of the work;
- subcontracting the bits clients do not see;
- training clients to do some of the work themselves.

Students

Postgraduate students can provide 'intellectual manpower' on a project basis. They can be recruited through most universities and you can often find someone researching in your field of work. There are also opportunities to recruit students for longer assignments with the cost subsidized by a grant.

16 Surprises

predict and overcome unexpected hurdles

10 surprises that employees spring and how to overcome them

Being a boss is one of the most rewarding but often the most daunting aspects of building a business. Ideally, if your business is quite small, you will be both boss and buddy. Sometimes though, you get surprised. Here are ten common surprises.

1. **Coming in late every day** – what's changed at home to make mornings difficult? Partying every night? Find out and offer to help.

2. **Private phone calls** – remember the importance of give and take. Is enough extra being done to justify latitude? If so, say nothing.

3. **Pilfering** – if you take home stationery, materials and more you are setting a bad example. If employees see you doing this, they will think they can too.

4. **Theft** – if someone's robbing you or your business call the police. Never compromise.

5. **BO** – it sounds trivial but a worker with a personal hygiene problem is one of the stickiest issues most bosses have to face. Encourage peer pressure to play on the pong; it's usually the best route.

6. **Moonlighting** – some specialists, for example graphic designers, take it as read that they can work for you in the day and themselves in the evening. Make your policy clear when you hire people. Avoid misunderstanding.

7. **Overfamiliarity** – as your business grows, so too must the distance between you and your staff. The fact is there will simply be more things you cannot share. Manage the gap.

8. **Sickies** – it's always useful to record sick leave and check for patterns. Is it on the increase? Do days off coincide with job interviews elsewhere?

9. **Different values** – we all have to be tolerant of the views of employees. But when every last yoghurt carton has to be recycled and skimmed organic milk is all they will take in their fair trade coffee, you begin to wonder. Check their values before you hire; it saves all sorts of hassle later.

10. **Religion** – we live in a multicultural society and some people will decide not to undertake certain duties for religious reasons. Find out at interview, but with religious issues the keyword is tolerance.

Employment tribunals await those accused of discriminating against their employees. The fact is that when things go 'legal' everyone loses out. Negative publicity, workplace tension and the hassle and frustration of the process can all cause lasting damage to your business.

The art of avoiding workplace conflict is to prevent it ever happening. You can do this by:

- taking up references before you hire someone;

- asking about interests, beliefs and values at interview;

- trusting your instincts;

- setting out the ground rules in detail in an employee handbook;

- having professionally written contracts of employment.

If your business operates in a particularly sensitive area, for example medical research or meat production, you need to make doubly sure you have every angle covered before you hire staff. It is not unknown for journalists to pose as workers and, then expose what they present as bad practices.

CEDRIC

A fourth generation dairy farmer, Cedric hired a young lad who lived in the nearby town who had not worked on the land before. He reckoned that his cowman could teach the lad all he needed to know and being honest, felt he was rescuing the boy from inner city life and giving him a chance to work in the fresh air.

However, Cedric soon found out that some of the practices his family had followed for more than a hundred years were not looked on kindly by a pair of urban eyes. His new employee reported him to the RSPCA for cruelty and the local press reporting was not at all complimentary.

10 surprises that customers spring and how to overcome them

You can never plan for the unexpected. Here are ten common surprises that customers can deliver to spoil your day.

1. **Lost deliveries** – if you do not get deliveries signed for and a copy kept, there's nothing to stop your customers' staff pinching goods and saying they never arrived.

2. **Rampant returns** – you also need to make sure that someone checks and signs to verify that the goods are OK. Shortcomings on your customer's part can lead to problems that you get blamed for.

3. **Cash crisis** – you deliver weekly, and suddenly the customer is unable to pay. Do you keep supplying and hope they trade back to profit? Or cut deliveries, kill their business and lose out? It's usually best to cut your losses and pull out.

4. **Legislation** – someone reads of a new regulation and guess what, it means you have to do something in a different way. Make sure you pass on the cost.

5. **Relationships** – your salesman has been sleeping with their buyer and her husband has just found out. You've probably lost a customer!

6. **Crime** – your fastest growing customer has been jailed for fraud. Can you jump in and take the customers he can no longer service?

7. **Complaints** – sometimes people make promises that your product or service cannot deliver. Provide data sheets that specify what you can guarantee.

8. **Goodbye** – you've done everything possible at great expense, then you are dropped in favour of somebody else. Make sure you ask why and act on the feedback.

9. **Pay twice** – their accounts person has a bad day and you get paid twice. The end of year audit will inevitably reveal the mistake, so send the cheque back now and score a point for honesty.

10. **Offer cash** – money laundering and the black economy are two activities no self-respecting business should get involved in. Rather like illicit drugs, after the first episode it's almost impossible to turn back.

Consultants and others selling their time can also have problems managing customers' expectations. Here are some common problems that befall such hapless consultants.

- **Over-promising** – in the excitement of doing the deal, you agree to solve all their problems. Trouble is, this is like painting the Forth Bridge; the task continues long after the budget runs out. You are seen to have failed.

- **Poor diagnosis** – if a consultant only addresses the symptoms presented, disaster can often result. Diagnosing the true issue and sorting that out is what you have to do.

- **Terms of reference** – define the parameters of the project so that both parties understand. Only then can you be sure that you have finished the task.

- **Dependency** – poor consultants create client dependency. They do a job for you but never solve the underlying problem. Always treat the cause, not the symptoms.

- **Personal prejudice** – respect for clients, their views, value and ideals, is vital for a successful relationship. Do not impose your values on their business.

NORMAN

A graphic designer, Norman agreed to do a job for cash. He figured this would be good because it would save him tax and allow him to be generous with his friends on Saturday night.

When the client came to collect the work and pay up, Norman was out. The client popped the £300 in the only envelope she could find, a pre-paid direct mail response envelope from a magazine.

Norman came home and posted the envelope, thinking his secretary was responding to the mailshot. When he realized his mistake he chose to stay at home on Saturday night and sulk. He never undertook 'cash jobs' again.

10 surprises that suppliers spring and how to overcome them

Your suppliers may regard you as their best customer, but they may still let you down. Here are ten common surprises that suppliers can deliver to spoil your day.

1. **Lost deliveries** – the goods really do go astray and they cannot replace them. Make sure you keep a stock of all vital components.

2. **Quality drops** – if quality drops, work with them to resolve the problem. Visit them and see what is going wrong. Don't simply shout!

3. **Corporate deafness** – you've told them five times that something's wrong and they still keep doing it. Might mean it's time to find an alternative.

4. **Holiday** – make sure you know when suppliers are going on holiday and make sure you've got the gap covered.

5. **Price rises** – traditionally everyone passed on price rises, adding their own margin along the way. The end user picked up the eventual tab. Today there is more competition; don't accept price rises without debate.

6. **Service stops** – if you stick with products that become outdated, be aware that unless you buy enough, your supplier might find it uneconomic to continue supplying you.

7. **Over-engineering** – any product or service can be over-engineered by the purist supplier. Don't fund their pride; make sure they work down to your price, not up to the highest possible standard.

8. **Legislation** – as with customers, the rules concerning suppliers can change and scupper what you've enjoyed for years. Watch the horizon for new regulations.

9. **Going bust** – sometimes suppliers go bust. Make sure you're not reliant on one supplier and if the worst happens consider not paying the last bill. Often, liquidators will not pursue an insolvent company's creditors.

10. **Soured friendship** – be cautious of enjoying too much of your supplier's hospitality. Sometimes, the friendship that develops is compromised by work.

Choosing suppliers for your business is not as easy as you might think. Try to:

- buy on quality, innovation and service as well as price;
- credit-check suppliers to make sure they're secure;
- take references from satisfied customers;
- let them make a profit too;
- write down the agreed 'service level agreement' so everyone understands.

Service level agreements sound grand but, in fact, are no more than documents that define:

- each aspect of the working relationship;
- what both parties have agreed to do;
- the penalties for failing to deliver;
- how the relationship will develop;
- how success is reviewed and improvement sought.

BARRY

Although now retired, Barry tells a wonderful, if sobering, story from when he was site manager running a major agrochemical manufacturing plant. Being the only chemical plant in the city, there were no similar businesses nearby so some specialist suppliers were difficult to find locally.

One particular firm handled all of Barry's 'high pressure' stainless steel repair work and the plant became dependent on their quick, local service. The firm encountered financial problems and Barry was faced with possibly losing a key supplier. He arranged for some of his management team to work with the supplier through the difficult patch. The supplier survived and the relationship is now even closer.

10 sleepless nights you can probably avoid

It's too easy to worry about just about everything. Here are ten things that might happen but probably never will.

1. **Jury service** – if summoned to join a jury, you are usually allowed to be excused once if you really cannot spare the time. Most people never get called.

2. **Crime** – as long as you have a security system and are sensible, your business is unlikely to be attacked. Keep data backups off site though, just in case.

3. **Health** – looking after your health and insuring the obvious risks will ensure that poor health is unlikely to damage your business.

4. **Hacking** – apart from credit card fraud, you are unlikely to be of interest to hackers. They tend to target big organizations.

5. **Divorce** – remembering that divorce can cost you half your company and make domestic life far from comfortable, it makes sense to dedicate time and effort to keeping your relationship on an even keel.

6. **War** – unless you or your team are reservists, even a full-scale war is unlikely to take people away from your workplace.

7. **Terrorism** – does your business operate in sensitive locations? If not, don't worry. If yes, take advice.

8. **Bankruptcy** – you will probably find enough work for next month and there are umpteen stages of decline before financial apocalypse. Don't panic!

9. **Strikes** – even if your workers are ardent members of a trade union, industrial action is unlikely to disrupt your business if you are fair, open and honest.

10. **Death** – some people worry about dying and what would happen to the business. Relax, in this eventuality it's someone else's problem!

Fear, reality and risk

In our dark moments, when tired, stressed and anxious, the world seems far more likely to deliver your enterprise a deadly blow than when you're on a roll.

Remember these things.

- Reality is:
  - where you are right now;
  - your replay of what usually happens to others;
  - a world where there is time to plan, think and react.

- Fear is:
  - irrational;
  - brought on by unlikely events you might face;
  - delivered most often to those that invite it.

- Risk is:
  - measurable;
  - insurable;
  - manageable.

Focusing on risk is sensible when you are planning but damaging if you think about it all the time. Remember the 80:20 rule – spend most of your time on the 20% of your activities/customers/products that carry 80% of your opportunity.

> HENRY is a potter with his own gallery. In the past five years he has managed to:
>
> - dry himself out with the help of alcoholics anonymous;
> - get divorced;
> - see a good friend die young;
> - seen his savings dwindle to zero.
>
> Despite all these knocks he remains bullish and confident about his businesses future. He knows that life can be tough, but equally he knows that bad is never too bad when you're actually there. If Henry can manage, so can you.

17 Helpers

people who might help you, or hinder you

10 people eager to help you succeed

Many people are only too willing to offer you their advice. Remember though, it's your business, your money and your livelihood. Here are ten kinds of people you might meet and advice as to how to handle them.

1. **Mum** – as with anyone who truly loves you, unless successful entrepreneurs themselves, treat any business advice offered with caution.

2. **Bank** – always remember that banks are in business for themselves and, increasingly, want to sell you more of their services. That said, banks do offer sound general advice that is well worth heeding.

3. **Accountant** – ideal if you are risk averse, accountants are brilliant at helping to reduce costs, but usually unimaginative when it comes to increasing sales.

4. **Financial advisers** – independent and trusted, friendly financial advisers can occupy a useful position. They are less biased than a bank, more entrepreneurial than most accountants. Good guys to talk to when you need to raise cash.

5. **Consultants** – consultants charge for their time. Your challenge is to extract value from that time. With a good brief, consultants can provide great advice. But, ask a silly question . . .

6. **Friends** – might only want to play out their business dreams with your business. Friends usually have the best shoulders for crying on.

7. **Customers** – always listen to your customers. They need you to succeed and are well placed to offer advice.

8. **Suppliers** – involving your suppliers in your business development is a good way to get introduced to their own innovation. They might even pay you to test new things.

9. **Support agencies** – there's a whole world of government-funded business advice out there. Much of it is good and almost all of it is independent and sincere. Jump through their 'red tape' hoops and they'll help you no end.

10. **Yourself** – yes, you are probably your own best-qualified business adviser. Listen to your intuition and take time to reflect on what your experience tells you.

Choosing a business adviser

Whoever you choose to share your challenges with, make sure they have all or some of the following characteristics:

- **Empathy** – on your wavelength as a human being.
- **Knowledge** – of your business sector.
- **Interest** – in your challenge, not just money motivated.
- **Enthusiasm** – and a willingness to explore new ideas with you.
- **Contacts** – with other people able to help you make it happen.
- **Open mind** – rather than having the attitude 'one solution fits all'.
- **Track record** – successful, but not necessarily as a consultant.
- **Ethics** – so you won't be led to places you find uncomfortable.
- **Wealth** – if your adviser has not made much money their advice could be suspect.
- **Radar** – the ability to see what's just over your business horizon.

When preparing a brief for your adviser, remember to include:

- an overview of what your business does;
- your vision for the future;
- the key issues you feel you are facing;
- how you feel an adviser can help;
- your budget and what you expect to see from your investment.

MARTIN

Nearing retirement age, Martin has enjoyed a long and successful senior management career. No longer working full-time, he now enjoys helping others to succeed in business as well as he has over the years. Comfortably off, the fees he charges reflect more the ability of his client to pay, than his desire to dramatically boost his income.

Martin works with those he finds interesting and where he knows his experience and skill will add the most value. He has a great network and acts as a 'general practitioner' for his clients, introducing others as the need arises.

There are many people like Martin out there in most large towns. All you have to do is find him or her.

10 things consultants do well

However hard you try, it's really difficult to remain objective when you are so close to the coalface. A good consultant can help you see and deal with the blockages every business has. Here are ten examples.

1. **Marketing** – communicating your strengths to prospective customers requires specialist expertise. Few fail to benefit from help in this area.

2. **Innovation** – doing old things in new ways, or simply doing new things, requires you to stop long enough to think. Consultants give you the time and they have been there before.

3. **Cost control** – a fresh pair of eyes can often see clearly where profits are leaking from your company.

4. **Funding** – finding the money to grow needs a combination of accountancy skills and a good knowledge of the funding playing field. What's more, lenders may actually have more confidence in the consultant than you!

5. **Recruitment** – choosing the right people is often better done by others. After all, recruitment consultants do it all the time.

6. **Training** – reconciling your business needs with the skills available and planning how to plug the gaps is crucial. Why not get an expert to help?

7. **Firing** – it may seem a cop-out but if you've got a problem member of staff then a specialist in employment law can help sort it out.

8. **IT** – technology is constantly changing. Make sure someone is keeping you up to date.

9. **Property** – whether buying, selling, building, altering or adapting most people get outside help with sorting out property issues.

10. **Health** – you should plan regular private health consultations to make sure you and your key people are in tip-top order.

Consultants are like cars – they come in all shapes and sizes and there's usually a choice within your price range. As with cars, it's no good buying a cheap one if you want to make a long journey. Equally, the top of the range model might be good for your ego, but if you simply want to potter around the block it's a bit of a waste. Here are some places you might look to find a consultant.

- **Ask a friend** – to recommend someone they've been happy with.

- **Support agencies** – have lists of vetted consultants who they know can do the job.

- **Accountants** – usually know who can deliver and who to avoid.

- **Networks** – generate many useful contacts.

- **Professional bodies** – often have experts in the field you are exploring.

Consultants tend to come in two types, strategists and tacticians. Here's how to choose between them.

Strategists	Tacticians
Help you decide where to go	Grab your hand and take you there
Write impressive reports	Write impressive operational plans
Are often academically gifted	Often have battle scars
Can rarely help you deliver their plan	Can implement but not write the plan

10 things to share, not buy

Why do we all buy things we hardly use? Think how much more profitable your business could be if you shared stuff instead? Here are ten things you could share.

1. **Machines** – why not club together with neighbours and share the forklift truck?

2. **People** – help others when they are pushed and you are quiet. They will reciprocate when deadlines threaten to crush you!

3. **Postal collection** – share a franking machine and have the postman pick up your mail from one convenient point. Share the cost, enjoy the convenience.

4. **Learning** – lend good books to those around you. Take up spare places on training courses.

5. **Suppliers** – buy together in bulk for bigger discounts.

6. **Customers** – cross sell, for example introduce others to your customers and they'll recommend you to theirs.

7. **Intelligence** – keep the jungle drums beating on your business park. Don't keep hot intelligence to yourself; share it out.

8. **Canteen** – everyone has to eat, but at work most people make do with eating sandwiches at their desk. Create a shared canteen with other firms and network as you nosh.

9. **Security** – neighbourhood watch schemes in business areas can reduce insurance costs and prevent crime. Ask the police for information.

10. **Waste** – recycling and the prevention of pollution can be an expensive headache. Share the challenge with others; ask your local council to help.

Good neighbours

Creating a friendly, supportive business environment is good for everyone. Too often, business estates are littered with barriers and barbed wire – each enterprise forming an oasis of activity in a desert of weeds, litter and abandoned supermarket trolleys. Consider:

● hosting a meeting of nearby business owners to discuss how to improve the shared environment;

- organizing lunchtime litter patrols;

- planting trees;

- signage that helps visitors find the business they're looking for, and discover others too;

- starting a 'best kept factory' award scheme in your neighbourhood.

LINDA

For ten years, Linda has managed a machinery ring in Caithness. More than 130 farmers pay an annual membership fee and ring Linda when they need help on the farm. 'Most are one man bands', Linda said, 'so sometimes they need manpower as well as machines. I ring round and find what they need from someone who has the time or equipment. The machinery ring takes a commission for arranging each job.'

If the machinery ring did not exist these farmers would each need to buy their own machinery. By offering labour as well, farmer's sons, who might otherwise have had to leave the land, can work at home and for neighbours.

Machinery rings are common in farming communities. Could your business community do something similar?

10 things you can often put off until later

Building a business means you are constantly bombarded by new opportunities. Usually they involve your time and your money. You can't do it all at once, so here's a list to help you decide what to leave for later.

1. **ISO 9000** – you get to a stage where systems really appeal. But be sure there is a commercial benefit to being assessed against external standards before you say yes.

2. **Investors in people** – this is a standard which indicates how well your business goals and team development plans are aligned. Doing it is important; being assessed maybe less so.

3. **Buying a big car** – you need to give yourself treats when the business does well, but is it doing that well right now? If so, buy it; if not . . . well, take a test drive and plan to deserve it soon.

4. **Moving premises** – moving is very expensive and disruptive. Delay it by homeworking, hot-desking or installing a mezzanine floor.

5. **Hiring people** – if the workload is not rising steadily consider covering the peaks with temporary, freelance or agency staff.

6. **Advertising** – networking and referrals are the best ways to win new customers. Exhaust these avenues before advertising.

7. **Retiring** – if you no longer want to run your business, hire a general manager to do it for you. The right person might one day buy you out!

8. **Insurance** – every business needs insurance, but some risks are very small. You must insure your vehicles but do you really need to cover the cost of a major tax investigation?

9. **Taking dividends** – well done if you delay taking out more than you actually need. Growth takes lots of cash and it's always better to avoid having to put back what you've taken out!

10. **Holidays** – to be effective you should always take holidays; but you already knew that didn't you?

Deciding when to do new or different things is largely a matter for your own judgement. The trouble is that if you ask your advisers, family and friends they will all offer different advice. Decision making is a key skill the successful entrepreneur needs to develop. Here are some ways to ease indecision.

- **Benchmark** – this is a clever way of saying measure your business against other people's. In other words, see how others have dealt with the issue and learn from their experience. There is little that hasn't been seen before!

- **Whiteboard** – invest in a large whiteboard and use it to sketch out alternative scenarios. Use it to develop your thinking.

- **Sleep on it** – there are people who swear that if the last thing you think about before going to sleep is a big decision then you will wake with the answer. It sounds corny, but it often works.

- **Mentor** – a good mentor will listen and encourage as you talk yourself through the options. Friends can do this, but only if they stay objective.

- **Third option** – look for the option you've yet to discover, let alone consider. This forces you to look at the existing options in a new way. Try it!

IAN

A direct descendent of landscape gardener Capability Brown, Ian's family have always worked the land. When his father died suddenly Ian, just 21, took over the holding that the family had occupied for generations. He soon found that everything in their garden was far from rosy. Losing money, with big debts and at the mercy of world market prices for his crops, he knew he had to make some radical decisions.

After battling for several years, he signed up for an MBA at Durham Business School and gained a wider perspective on his options. An innovative deal with his landlord meant that he gave back the land he had been farming, but retained the buildings. He created what is now an award winning business park. He now farms businesses not crops, and has found this far more lucrative.

18 Balance

when to work and when to play

10 signs that you are getting stressed

Business life can be pretty unforgiving. It's not surprising that stress is far more common than you might think among people running their own business. Here are ten common symptoms that work is beginning to get you down.

1. **Headaches** – if you are reaching for the headache pills more and more often, it might mean you're doing too much.

2. **Butterflies** – are important if you are to perform well in important meetings, but if everything you face prompts that familiar flutter . . .

3. **Coffee** – fuels most of our days, but are you drinking more and more?

4. **Booze** – can take you away from your problems, but only for a while.

5. **Paranoia** – you are beginning to feel oppressed. Is the world really plotting your downfall? Or are you imagining the worst?

6. **In bed** – you might notice that two things are more difficult to manage. One is sleep; the other you can guess at and it affects men more than women!

7. **Wind** – this could also be a problem in bed, but when you're stressed you really do suffer more from flatulence!

8. **Poor judgement** – if you are stressed, your ability to make decisions is hampered. The consequences can be stressful in themselves.

9. **Waterfalls** – as the pace of life hots up you are in the loo almost every hour.

10. **Feedback** – you get that growing feeling that those around you are finding you difficult to deal with, increasingly irrational and generally bad company.

Many of the physical symptoms of stress occur in response to the production of adrenaline, perhaps compounded by your intake of caffeine, tobacco and alcohol. While we all have panic attacks from time to time (and that's a normal part of business life) stress is something different. Stress levels can rise gradually so that you hardly notice the change. The result is that your effectiveness falls and you become less user-friendly. Both make it harder to achieve the goals you set yourself.

There are countless books, websites and other sources of advice dealing with stress. To get you started, here are a few tips that can help you avoid getting unduly stressed.

- **Realism** – set out to perform well but do not be overambitious or set unrealistic goals.

- **Prioritize** – do today what has to be done today. Delegate as much as you are able and don't fret about tomorrow's task today.

- **Exercise** – however busy you are make time for regular physical exercise in your working week. Exercising also provides good thinking time.

- **Share** – we all need a confidant; someone you know you can discuss things with openly who will be supportive and help you see things as they really are.

- **Measure** – compare your firm's progress with your targets and the performance of those around you. Keep things in perspective.

Getting help

If stress is your problem, seek help. A search of the internet or local telephone directory will point you towards:

- charities that provide counselling and support for stress and mental illness;

- professionals who, for a fee, will help you unpick and resolve the issue;

- gyms where you can work out your stress and take time out.

Unresolved stress can damage your health, both physically and mentally. Don't let it!

10 ways to enjoy your work

Work–life balance is a popular concept, particularly with those who want to see us enjoy ourselves without compromising our business. Of course, it is far easier to say than to achieve. Here are ten ways to have fun at work.

1. **Staff outing** – set some shared targets and organize a trip to celebrate their achievement. Get to know your people through play as well as work.

2. **Business park outing** – if you work alone why not take those who work in neighbouring units instead? Learn how you can collaborate with them.

3. **Buy toys** – invest in new technology perhaps before you really need it. Appreciate the way it makes your life simpler as well as more enjoyable.

4. **Plant a garden** – think how impressed your customers will be if that scruffy corner is filled with flowers. Now you can hold summer meetings outdoors.

5. **Hire pictures** – did you know you can hire as well as buy art? Keep an ever-changing collection of original pictures to brighten every day.

6. **Open windows** – a stuffy environment can make you drowsy. Let the fresh air in, and perhaps even listen to the birds from your desk.

7. **Play sport** – challenge your customers and others to a friendly game. Do some selling afterwards over a beer.

8. **Sponsor someone** – link your company with someone's world-beating attempt. Link their challenge to one of your own and donate more if you win your business race too.

9. **Try trains** – next time you travel on business, take the train and leave the car at home. Miss the traffic and read a novel.

10. **Take work home** – not usually a recipe for balance, unless you do it during normal working hours. Create quiet times when you can plan.

We are all conditioned to think that work is work and life is something different. For true entrepreneurs there is no distinction between the two. That is not to say they work all the time, more that they probably enjoy each of the week's activities equally. Established, successful entrepreneurs:

- love everything they do;

- forget what makes money and what does not;

- ignore weekends and are just as likely to play in the week;
- overlook that others sometimes have to fit in with others;
- dress confidently knowing that no one can impose rules.

You will know that you are successful and have arrived when:

- money becomes a want, not a need;
- recognition by others becomes important;
- giving help to others makes you as happy as helping yourself;
- others seek you out with their ideas and opportunities;
- banks give you back the loan guarantees you made earlier.

RICHARD

Now in his mid 50s, Richard has worked hard to build up his business. To his delight, his son Will asked a couple of years ago if he could leave his job and come home to help run the firm. Will soon made his mark and proved he could manage the business day to day, freeing up Richard's time to explore new business opportunities.

Richard has become active in several local business networks and industry training initiatives. He really enjoys helping others go through the stages of business growth he experienced as a younger man. To his surprise, this willingness to give has raised his profile locally and led to his company winning new clients. Richard is a very content entrepreneur.

10 holiday ideas for when you can't afford to take time off

Experts tell us that several short breaks can be as refreshing as three weeks on the beach. Here's ten ways to squeeze holidays into your busy schedule.

1. **Long weekends** – leave the office at 3pm on Friday and go somewhere exciting. Monday will be really productive if you've been away for the weekend.

2. **Volunteer** – if you help with a youth or other group, you can take trips that actually build your local reputation. This is valuable if you retail.

3. **Extra days** – if you're travelling on business, take an extra day to see the sights. Take your partner with you to reconnoitre while you are working.

4. **An hour's enough** – even if only going locally, an extra hour to walk, shop or sit in the park with an ice cream will make all the difference.

5. **Join the army** – the various volunteer reserve forces can give you excellent free training in your spare time and trips to new places too. Learn, earn and play all at the same time.

6. **Cook a meal** – even if you cannot spare any time off, you can take the time to read a recipe book in the morning, shop in the afternoon and prepare your partner a surprise meal in the evening. Over dinner talk about holidays!

7. **Entertain** – while no one does the blow-out corporate lunches experienced (or endured!) by many in the 1980s, a convivial evening with a customer at the theatre or football match allows you to combine work with time off.

8. **Think technology** – if you really cannot bear to be out of touch, move your office to your holiday destination. Call forwarding and internet access mean you can sit by the pool and work as if at your desk.

9. **Pretend you're sick** – imagine you've broken your leg; organize cover at work and take a holiday. Do not break your leg.

10. **Take a walk!** – a lunchtime walk to the travel agent's office is one short break that might lead to another!

Holidays are actually great business opportunities. You should not need an excuse to take time out to enjoy yourself. Here are more reasons why holidays are important.

- **Inspiration** – see how you can take ideas from other areas back to your business.

- **Networking** – get to know other holidaymakers; are they potential clients?

- **Blue sky** – clear your mind, watch the clouds and imagine.

- **Seek novelty** – regulations vary across the globe. See how others do what you do.

- **Challenge your thinking** – experience the extreme and put your worklife in perspective.

IAN

Ian worked in the food industry so took a great interest in what he saw in American supermarkets while on holiday. He saw a healthy snack product sold for children's lunchboxes that seemed very popular.

After detailed research, he started a business in England making similar products and has watched his business grow. If he hadn't gone on holiday he would have missed the opportunity.

19 Philanthropy

how to help yourself by helping others

10 ways to build your business by helping others

Whilst altruism is to be commended, helping others usually only becomes sustainable when there is an equal benefit to you or your organization. Here are ten things you can do to help yourself by helping others.

1. **Mentor** – mentoring someone less experienced than yourself keeps you in touch with reality.

2. **Donate product** – if you make a consumer product, give it away free to outlets where others will see it and buy it as a result.

3. **Speak** – share your experience and advice with groups containing potential customers, suppliers, employees, etc. Speaking at such events builds your profile and represents free marketing.

4. **Case study** – volunteer to be a case study for a supplier or support agency. They will then promote you by sending the case study to people you don't yet know.

5. **Host visits** – allow others to see how you run your firm to encourage them to do business with you.

6. **Share surpluses** – otherwise wasted materials and capacity can be given to needy groups winning valuable publicity.

7. **Teach kids** – explaining what you do and why to a group of 13 year olds is a great experience. It will certainly make you think because kids ask lots of questions and demand credible answers.

8. **Run a competition** – offer something your business does as a prize in a fund-raising draw. Offer those who do not win a discount.

9. **Put a bench outside your shop** – make it possible for people to rest outside your shop. It makes it look busier and everyone will look in the window.

10. **Advertise** – in places where your customers go. For example, a coach holiday company might restore the town centre bus stop and include an advert for its own services.

As soon as you recognize that your business forms part of a wider society, you begin to see that the opportunities are endless. The concept of helping to raise your firm's profile through helping others is perhaps a little more complex than those embodied in some of the other checklists. To help you get the point here are some specific examples of things that some businesses have done.

Activity	Benefit to the business
Baker gives leftover cakes to hostel for rough sleepers	Everyone knows the cakes they buy are really fresh
Accountant runs free advice sessions for start-up businesses	This is the first accountant the new entrepreneur meets; they'll probably come back
An ad agency does all the marketing for a city charity appeal for nothing	Their work is seen by more people and they get lots of press coverage
An engineering works allows a local college to train students in its workshops after hours	Students get to spend time in a potential employer's environment; ' The employer can also 'talent spot'
IT training company helps in a school	Parents consider how the company could raise their skill levels

10 ways to entertain your customers for free

Creating social opportunities to bond with those we want to trade with can be difficult. Many prefer not to accept corporate gifts and the days of lavish lunches are long past. Here are ten politically correct and free ways to entertain customers.

1. **Fund-raising dinner** – people will buy tickets for a dinner if some of the money goes to a good cause. People will also be more likely to attend!

2. **Join a club** – even if you are not into 'gentleman's clubs', you can join something that provides appropriate hospitality opportunities. For example, friends of art galleries can take guests to exhibitions for free.

3. **Ask them to pay!** – if they recognize that you have pared your costs to the bone and have made only a modest profit, then why shouldn't they buy lunch for you?

4. **Supplier visit** – get your supplier to fund factory visits. Offer the trip to those who increase their sales with you.

5. **Trade body events** – take your customer to hear industry pundits at trade events.

6. **Recognize achievement** – give an award for excellence in your field. Invite others to the presentation. Have the buffet sponsored by your bank.

7. **Take them on a walk** – perhaps not viewed by all as entertaining, but encouraging your customers to join you in a sponsored walk will certainly help all to get to know each other better.

8. **Hijack a trade seminar** – organize your own 'fringe' programme around an event you and your customers are attending. It's cheaper than doing it on your own.

9. **Travel together** – people seem reluctant to car share yet offering a lift to those you want to influence, when you are both going to a trade show for example, converts travelling time into selling time.

10. **Give kittens** – If your cat surprises you by having babies, ask your customers to provide good homes to the kittens. You always then have something to talk about when you ring them up.

Fund-raising events can create fantastic opportunities to bring together customers, prospects, suppliers and others important to your success. As suggested in the checklist, those you invite will buy their ticket and pay their way. They might also provide raffle and tombola prizes. These events take a lot of organizing and the benefiting good cause should be able to help. Here are some other benefits to fund-raising events:

- big name speakers will often waive their fee if they approve of the cause;
- people will come to network with each other – they will talk about you;
- guests of guests are often new people you've never met;
- you get plenty of profile and get to speak to everyone;
- the presentation of the cheque may be featured in the press;
- following up to make sure people enjoyed themselves will lead to talking business;
- others may sponsor certain elements of the event so you can raise more money;
- sharing the event with a non-competitor lets you influence each other's networks;
- invitations can carry subtle advertising;
- everyone thinks you're a generous person – this makes business easier to do.

LEN

A haulier with a fleet of tipper trucks and hire skips, Len does not have a sophisticated business, nor is it particularly important to any of his customers. Few would choose to socialize with him.

Recognizing this, he organized a charity barbecue in his yard with food, music and a guest celebrity. He planned to raise money for the local hospice. He invited everyone he had ever dealt with offering tickets at £20 per head.

200 people bought tickets and most turned up. His costs were £10 per head so he was able to present the hospice with a cheque for £2,000. Parked around the outside of his yard was his fleet of trucks. People said they had not realized how large and modern his fleet was. On Monday morning he booked jobs for three new customers – each had been a guest at the barbecue. As Len mused, 'why advertise when they will pay to come and see what I do?'

10 special things about family businesses

Family firms are special. They are often structured to give long-term wealth to an ever-growing family. They also face rather special challenges. Here are ten of the best.

1. **Making room** – after a few generations, your family firm may be full of family members expecting a job for life. Let them all own shares but only employ those with the skills and aptitude the business needs.

2. **Cash or custody?** – often, each generation is seen as the caretaker and not encouraged to take risks or sell out. Are your relatives best served by holding shares or having the money?

3. **Genes or jeans** – being family should never be the only reason why someone is employed in the firm. Offer jobs outside and be objective when recruiting.

4. **Table talk** – respect the access you may have to the business patriarch over Sunday lunch. Envious or distrustful colleagues will hold you back. Be one of the team as well as one of the family.

5. **Inheritance** – you need specialist tax planning advice with a family firm if the expectation is to pass it on to future generations.

6. **Spare the rod** – you can also try too hard not to favour your offspring at work. Do not make the mistake of discriminating against them.

7. **No moles** – encouraging a family member to report back on employees, or vice versa, will wreck the working relationship in the team.

8. **Avoid big treats** – if you want to buy your daughter, who works in the firm, a £30,000 sports car, make sure that everyone knows it's not a company perk.

9. **New ventures** – create opportunities for your newly recruited child to build their own business within yours. This makes it easier for their success to stand out.

10. **Be lateral** – why not take profits from your business and invest in one of your children?

Many books have been written about family firms for they form a significant part of most economies. The problems that researchers and advisers observe tend to result from:

- family arguments that move from home to work;

- couples who live and work together having no time apart;

- divorce;

- reluctance to discipline or dismiss when performance falls short;

- creating jobs for people, rather than creating jobs and recruiting for them.

Families that work together do have some considerable strengths, particularly in times of adversity. Look at how farmers deal with economic downturn. They:

- draw out only the money they need to live (often less than the minimum wage);

- consolidate neighbouring businesses by intermarrying to create a larger unit;

- diversify, building on their resources to create linked ventures;

- take a long-term view, particularly if asset rich and cash poor;

- have a feeling of heritage and see themselves as custodians, not owners.

While most of us have no wish to make similar sacrifices, we can learn a lot from the way farmers adapt to the circumstances they encounter.

PHILIP

Determined not to work with his brothers in the family building firm, Philip started a contract cleaning business supplying, initially those within the family and social network. Within a few years, the business had grown to the extent that it employed more people than the family building business

Philip does not talk about the structure of the business, but it is likely that profits are shared between the brothers irrespective of their role in the businesses. Philip has been entrepreneurial in creating a bigger, more diverse enterprise for future generations.

10 ways to prune your business to keep it manageable

There's nothing wrong with deciding to keep your business to a manageable size – after all, you can't enjoy your success if you're working seven days a week. Here are ten things you might do.

1. **Bud off** – as your business grows, encourage it to divide like an amoeba. Each departing venture should give the shareholders some cash as it leaves.

2. **Create divisions** – this way you create autonomous businesses, each with its own management but ownership remains with you. Divisions need not be large; simply distinct and separate.

3. **Sell bits off** – encourage growing customers or suppliers to buy product groups, market share or other aspects of the business you can move out.

4. **Outsource** – contract others to do much of the work. This reduces your hassle but retains your interest in the future opportunity.

5. **Sell and leaseback** – more a way of releasing capital; but if you cannot afford to retire and the company is not currently easy to sell, liquidating assets might help you and the business (if you share the proceeds).

6. **Focus on the core** – wind up all those potential new ventures you explored that didn't quite make it, but that somehow have never gone away.

7. **Become choosy** – if you are good at what you do but just want to do less, become choosy and put your price up.

8. **Say no** – most true entrepreneurs find it almost impossible to say 'no' to work. Saying 'no' sometimes keeps life simple; is that what you want?

9. **Pareto** – the 80:20 rule says that 20% of your activity generates 80% of the results. Apply the principle to your business and see where you're wasting your time.

10. **Take a holiday** – when you are refreshed you might no longer want to cut back; instead you might find your entrepreneur's 'second wind' and grow some more.

As with any change you are planning, you may find it helpful to get an objective outside view. If downsizing is on your agenda you certainly won't want to seek the views of your team – your decision might affect their jobs. Here are some people you might ask for guidance.

- **Accountant** – who works out what is profitable and what is not.

- **Pension adviser** – who tells you how much you'd earn if you retired.

- **Business transfer agent** – who values the enterprise, as a whole and in parts.

- **Your family** – who might be waiting for you to invite them to join the firm.

- **Yourself** – why do you really want to limit the size of your enterprise?

Rather like a garden, businesses become lank and overgrown. Pruning every few years can be good. You clear out dead wood and rubbish, and generally tidy and focus the whole outfit. This is nothing more than good housekeeping and need not be linked to any desire on your part to downsize or prepare for sale or retirement.

SAM

An agricultural merchant, Sam's business had grown and diversified. He supplied seeds, traded grain, made animal feed and ran a fleet of lorries. When he was 55 his sons, who were established in their careers, decided they did not want to join their father's company. Sam decided to stop growing and start preparing for his retirement.

First to go was his feed milling operation. Needing investment, he closed the plant and commissioned a large firm with a huge mill to manufacture his feed for him. To his surprise, he actually made more money. Over the years, the transport went the same way and within five years he found himself with a lean business with low overheads, no debt and healthy profits. He was approached by a bigger merchant and sold out.

Five years previously, his business was too complex and too vulnerable to be of value to anyone else.

10 benefits of making a philanthropic gesture

The simple fact is that you cannot take your money with you when you die. It makes sense, therefore, to be philanthropic with the profits your business generates. Entrepreneurs really can make a difference. Here's ten reasons why you should.

1. **Feel good** – using the proceeds of your success to help others makes you feel good.

2. **Lasting** – however big a name you have in your business sector, you will soon be forgotten when you sell, retire or die; harsh, but true. Giving buys a lasting legacy.

3. **Tax** – you need to take advice, but giving to charitable causes is incredibly tax efficient.

4. **Children** – some of the richest people choose to allow their children to generate their own wealth. They give their own wealth away rather than let their children bask in it.

5. **How much is enough?** – when you've made sufficient to realize your life's dreams, the rest just becomes an investment portfolio you worry about.

6. **World changing** – most investment in society's infrastructure is made with public money and decided by bureaucrats. After years of fighting bureaucracy, why stop when you've made your pile?

7. **Direct action** – money means you can make a difference to things you care about. It's more effective than lobbying.

8. **Vital** – some sectors, for example the arts, rely on patronage to survive.

9. **Recognition** – if this is important to you, most major gifts can be publicly acknowledged. Anonymity is preferred by some.

10. **Protection** – for things that might otherwise be lost for ever. It is a fact that increasingly, it is only philanthropy that keeps many worthwhile projects running.

There are as many philanthropic opportunities as there are people to satisfy them. However, as an entrepreneur you may be more interested in starting something yourself rather than simply responding to an appeal. Here are some ideas to get your mind working.

Area	Low budget	Medium budget	Massive budget
Education	Buy books for local school	Sponsor curriculum area	Build a school
	Provide an item of equipment	Equip a laboratory	Fund a university chair
Health	Provide a TV for the doctor's waiting room	Fund a specialist clinic	Build a hospice
	Provide an item of specialist equipment	Support work overseas	Build a medical mission
Arts	Pay for art therapy	Fund an arts worker	Build a gallery
	Sponsor an exhibition	Fund an 'artist in residence'	Fund a monument

PAUL

After many years as a senior manager, Paul led the management buyout of his division of a major food group. A few years later the business was sold on for more than three times the original purchase price. This made Paul a very wealthy man.

Perhaps in recognition of the important role his university education had played in his career success, Paul gave £8m to fund the creation of a management school that bears his name. Paul has made it easier for future generations of entrepreneurs to learn the business skills that he knows can make the difference between success and failure.

20 Exit

selling your successful business

10 ways to decide it's time to move on

A business should not be for life. There comes a time when it makes sense to move on. Here are ten signs to watch out for.

1. **You get an offer** – what could you do with both the money and the time? Review your life goals and discuss with your family what you should do.

2. **You're bored** – it happens; the business is no longer exciting and the problems seem to be greater than the opportunities.

3. **You're old** – why work longer than you really need to? There are no prizes for working into old age. Why not spend the kids' inheritance and enjoy it?

4. **Investment needed** – to stay competitive you need major investment and that would tie you in for a few years. If this is a re-run of an earlier experience you may prefer not to do it again.

5. **Market maturing** – you've had the best years and now it's time to adapt or perish. Alternatively, sell while there's still some market left.

6. **Big players?** – you've started in a niche market and grown to the point that the big players are getting annoyed. Maybe they'd like to buy you out?

7. **Opportunity knocks** – there's a great 'once in a lifetime' chance to get involved with something new. If you're sure it's not merely a case of 'grass looking greener' then sell to release time and cash.

8. **Eager beavers?** – your successor, who you've been grooming for years, is snapping at your heels. You may need to step aside at an appropriate time or you may lose out.

9. **Pressure at home** – there's nothing wrong with listening to your partner and finding more time to spend together. Many partners see a business as a love rival!

10. **You just want to** – if it feels right and you're sure it's what you want to do, then if you're the majority shareholder it's your prerogative to call the shots.

Moving on should ideally involve a clean break, both timewise and financially. It can be galling to witness others changing the way things are run. The fact is that no one is indispensable, not even you! It's also a fact of business life that every business should be on the market all the time. In other words, if the price is high enough you should always be receptive to offers.

When someone does buy your business, there may be attempts to tie you in as much as possible. This helps cash flow and more importantly, commits you to helping the business perform. You probably don't want this commitment.

When you respond to an offer, you need to negotiate a deal that gives you:

- **More up front** – it's better to take more money now and less later, rather than have your future wealth dictated by how the company, you no longer control, performs.

- **A quick exit** – some buyers want you to stick around for two years or more to manage the business under their ownership.

- **A fair deal** – you should not allow your greed to stop you getting a deal. Look forward, not back.

ANGUS

Having started a successful mail order retail business, Angus was flattered to be approached by a market leader. The company did not have a mail order division and recognized that buying one from Angus was preferable to building one from scratch.

The deal involved a lot of money but most of it was to be paid over the next few years and would depend on the division's performance. The deal also meant that Angus would have to stay on to run the business for a few years.

After much thought Angus turned the offer down. He didn't want to become an employee, nor did he want others to decide his payout for the profitability of his business as part of a group would be largely beyond his control.

10 things that add value to your business

Business transfer agents and accountants apply all sorts of formulae to value a business. The reality is that for most people the price you get when you sell is the price someone's prepared to pay. Here are ten business value boosters.

1. **Profits** – even if you've been milking the business and it only breaks even, the capability of the enterprise to line the owner's pockets is of prime importance.

2. **Potential** – can it get even bigger and better with additional investment, fresh enthusiasm and you off the scene? Hopefully yes!

3. **People** – if it's you and a bunch of halfwits you'll not get much. If, on the other hand you only need to pop in twice a week and have great people, the price increases.

4. **Premises** – is your business operating from a location that's worth more than the business itself? If your cycle repair shop could be bulldozed to make way for a supermarket, get excited.

5. **Property** – this is intellectual property. You need to protect anything that needs patenting (or otherwise protecting).

6. **Punters** – never underestimate the value of having a loyal bunch of repeat buyers. Inertia means they will probably stay when you've sold.

7. **Profile** – are you known as the best of the bunch? If your business has a positive profile, that's good. If it doesn't, work on it.

8. **Prima donna** – is a person seen as indistinguishable from their business. In other words, if you're indispensable the value will be lower.

9. **Position** – where you are physically located, together with your market position influences value. The more your business is seen to lead the better.

10. **Price** – we all have our price and few can resist an unexpected, generous offer. Be realistic if you're flattered by an approach.

Profits versus value

Hopefully, your business gives you a good income and a pleasing degree of control over how your spend your time. To be honest you can often achieve this as an employee, so why are you in business? The right answer is to create an enterprise that you can sell. This means that, at some point in the future, you can swap the overdraft for a pile of cash.

As you build your business, you should never lose sight of the need to add value and create an enterprise (or enterprises) that can be sold one day. This should be the carrot at the end of your stick. There are some personal qualities you need to develop if you are to build real value into your business. These include:

- Objectivity – you must let your head run your business, not your heart.

- Focus – stick to what you do best and do it better. Avoid distraction.

- Separate – the business is your baby but you need to give it room to be independent of you. Don't muddle up what's yours and what's the firm's.

MAURICE

A lifelong salesman, Maurice started a business at the age of 50 when he became fed up with working for others. His wife liked making soft toys and he started a business selling soft toy kits to independent haberdashers and chain stores.

He kept the business simple, renting a modern industrial unit and hiring agency staff to cut out and assemble kits. With an active social life and plenty of 'out of work' interests, he aimed to keep the business simple. A short product range and very low overhead costs meant that he could match demand closely with labour and thus his business was very profitable. When he decided to retire, all he really had to sell was a market share. The business was quickly acquired at a good price by a larger firm with spare production capacity.

People buy value, not costs!

10 ways to find a buyer

Clearly, if you hang a 'for sale' sign on the door customers, staff and suppliers will be inclined to worry. Here are ten ways to sell without making it obvious.

1. **Ask the accountant** – some accountants specialize in matchmaking between sellers and buyers of small businesses. They recruit buyers through seminars and local knowledge, and then broker the deal.

2. **Chat to suppliers** – if you sit between your suppliers and the marketplace, they might be interested in buying you out. Start the chat with 'just suppose'.

3. **Ask the team** – you will know your people well. Are they likely to be able to raise the cash?

4. **Box numbers** – you've seen the ads in the paper. They describe the business vaguely and give a box number for enquiries. It's cheap enough; try it!

5. **Rising stars** – who's the wunderkind in your sector? Would any patrons fund the purchase of your business? Treat to lunch and ask!

6. **Niggled neighbours** – you know you irritate the big players; you're faster, more flexible and often cheaper too. They might buy to close you down. Why not?

7. **Website** – for a few hundred pounds you can create a 'buy my business' website. You don't have to identify yourself, just make it appealing. Get the local newspaper to write about it and print the address.

8. **Agents** – as with houses and commercial property, there are agents who specialize in selling businesses.

9. **Insolvency practitioner** – these guys do not only work with companies that have failed. They are adept at extracting value from trading companies that otherwise might not be that attractive.

10. **Listen** – put yourself about and listen to what people say. If, for example, someone says how your market position is envied, explore their interest.

Working out what your business is worth has already been covered. It is essentially all about its potential to deliver future returns to the new owner. Your business will be worth more to someone who wants:

- **To buy it** – for maybe purely emotional reasons.

- **To plug a gap** – in their regional, national or international network.

- **More control** – of the market or supply chain.

- **Your people** – because they have valuable skills.

- **Your customers** – because winning them 'in battle' might cost more.

Selling up is not a quick process. Do not think of it as an escape route from an uncomfortable situation. It usually takes several months from the time you find your buyer to the cheque arriving. The buyer will want to delve deeply into your businesses affairs, accompanied usually by professional advisers. Make sure you have at least your accountant helping you through the process.

After you have sold your business you should never:

- dwell on the deal and question your decision;

- be envious if the business suddenly takes off;

- be smug if it consequently goes bust;

- compete with your former company;

- speak badly of the new team.

10 reasons to merge your business with another

One way to grow quickly, as well as create your own exit route, is to merge your business with another. When merging always make sure of these ten points.

1. **You'll get on** – really basic, but don't get yourself working with someone you don't feel comfortable with.

2. **2 + 2 = 5** – there has to be a clear benefit, either in terms of additional skills or reduced overhead costs; if 2 + 2 = 4, don't do it.

3. **Bigger is better** – if you are a minnow among sharks, then getting bigger quickly can protect you from being gobbled up and spat out.

4. **The figures add up** – take professional advice from your accountant, who will also check out the deal and protect your interests.

5. **Compliance costs** – some professional practices face ever-mounting compliance costs. Joining one or more together means you can share these costs.

6. **Knowledge base** – almost the opposite of compliance, but arguably more important in a fast-changing sector such as law or architecture, sharing your knowledge with others means both less spent and more learned.

7. **Customer overlap** – you supply the same people with different things. Merging means you have lots of time to find and service additional business.

8. **Premises** – your lease is running out and the other concern has space.

9. **Plant** – merging means you can buy one big efficient machine to do the work of two smaller inefficient ones.

10. **Love** – you'd be surprised how many businesses merge because the founders team up as a couple.

When you merge your business with another, only one person will remain top dog; businesses with two bosses rarely work. It will help therefore if one of the advantages of merging is that those leading the new business have complementary skills. One firm, for example, might be led by an accomplished salesperson who can win lots of new business. The other might be more delivery focused with the leader being an engineer or professional practitioner.

When merging two businesses you also need to check the following.

- **Employment contracts** – you will need to produce one that suits both teams.
- **Pay levels** – often these are different and they need to have parity.
- **Culture** – take the best of both businesses when creating your new one.
- **Your bank** – consult before doing the deal; this will be appreciated.
- **Customers** – make sure they're happy with what's planned.
- **Suppliers** – rationalize your list to retain the most supportive.
- **Employment law** – if there are to be casualties they should be dealt with fairly and in line with current best practice.
- **Guarantees** – make sure that you are sharing financial commitments fairly.
- **Perks** – if the other owner has a Porsche 'on the firm' and your car is more modest, you need to eliminate the danger of future disagreements.
- **Advisers** – if you have different advisers, collectively choose the one to stick with after the merger.

10 things you'll do differently the second time around

When you've sold your business, it might be a good idea to put into practice all you've learned and do it all again, either in the same business sector or a completely fresh one. There are ten ways in which you will probably be different.

1. **More objective** – separating better the desire to change the world and the urge to make money.

2. **People-focused** – the best businesses are those with the best people. Motivating others to deliver your vision is always easier the second time.

3. **Tougher** – we learn from our mistakes. Being tougher means taking no prisoners and focusing on results.

4. **Compassionate** – being aware of where others are trying to go makes you more tolerant and more willing to compromise a little.

5. **Better funded** – well, you've made some money haven't you?

6. **Better networked** – you know people and people know you. It's easier when you have an established network.

7. **Buy better** – this time, you've a track record so there will be plenty of choice.

8. **Sell more** – already successful, you know how to sell and will have a better hit rate than those just starting out.

9. **Play harder** – you've perhaps enjoyed a sabbatical and appreciate the value of quality time. Life is more balanced this time round.

10. **Quit quicker** – you'll build value faster and make your exit sooner.

Most businesses in the UK are small with annual sales of less than £150,000. Only a few experience the runaway success that can deliver vast riches. Running a small business is as much a career as a quest for wealth. As with a career, you will go further faster if you:

- **Move often** – selling, learning and starting again is the fastest way to grow.

- **Delegate** – focus more on strategy and less on operational issues.

- **Stay clean** – do not tarnish your reputation.

- **Help others** – it's odd, but the more you help others the better you do yourself.
- **Enjoy it** – making work fun makes it easier. This goes for your team too!

Really successful people often build a portfolio of businesses. These will include companies that they:

- **Invest in** – and support the executive team to achieve the vision.
- **Own** – but which are entirely managed by trusted employees.
- **Advise** – where they give their expertise freely and learn too.
- **Admire** – in which they have a small role but derive much pleasure.
- **Respect** – and want to help to succeed

To keep developing your skills as an entrepreneur you should now:

- scan business books and journals and read what's best for you;
- help others, for they in return will want to help you;
- listen to business speakers;
- keep a diary and in future, reflect on your past activities;
- share your knowledge, skill and expertise widely with others.

Robert Ashton

I hope you have found this book useful and have been prompted by the checklists and case studies to consider new ideas to launch or grow your business. This book is written for entrepreneurs like you as a starting point for the exploration of many challenges and opportunities.

When the book is updated and revised, it will contain new case studies that illustrate how readers like you have taken the ideas here and developed them to build profit and perhaps fun into their venture.

If you would like to be featured in the next edition, email me and describe how this book has helped you. Who knows, the publicity might help you as much as the book! I look forward to hearing from you.

robert@robertashton.co.uk
www.robertashton.co.uk

Contacts for case studies

Happy Drinking from The Entrepreneur's Book of Checklists and Virgin Wines!

Please enjoy this free £20 introductory voucher to spend with Virgin Wines.

Virgin Wines have hundreds of wines to choose from. Every one is guaranteed, has been reviewed and rated by real customers and is classified by how it tastes. You needn't be a wine expert - far from it - infact, their unique Wine Wizard can give recommendations personalised for you. You can mix your own or pick up a great value pre-mixed case and they'll deliver it straight to your door. As if that wasn't enough, their Customer Promise means that if you don't like a wine you don't pay.
And the best bit is that you can get £20 off your first case. Just follow the instructions below, sit back and wait for your wines. Go on...it'll save you loads of time, not to mention money!

You can use your introductory voucher to mix yourself a case of wine worth £50 or more, or buy one of Virgin Wine's great value mixed cases.

To use your voucher, go to <http://www.virginwines.com/slurp>, click on 'claim a voucher' and enter the voucher code and password below.

YOUR VOUCHER DETAILS
****

Voucher Code: EBOC

Password: champagne

****
You will need to spend your voucher by 31 December 2005
Please note: this voucher is for first time customers only, can only be used once and cannot be used in conjunction with any other promotional voucher or special case offers. This voucher can only be used against a case of wine (minimum 12 bottles of 75cl each) with a minimum value of £50 (excluding delivery of £4.99). You must be 18 to buy alcohol. Virgin Wines deliver anywhere in the UK, excluding Channel Islands and the Isle of Man. (See web site for full terms and conditions.)
****